With Hearts & Minds

Reflections on our participation in the Mass

Leader's Book

Acknowledgements

With Hearts & Minds - Reflections on our participation in the Mass - Leader's Book

Catholic Bishops' Conference of England and Wales - Liturgy Office.

Published 2005, by the Catholic Truth Society and Colloquium (CaTEW) Ltd.

The Catholic Truth Society, 40-46 Harleyford Road, Vauxhall, London SE11 5AY. *www.cts-online.org.uk*

Colloquium (CaTEW) Ltd, 39 Eccleston Square, London SW1V 1BX. *www.catholicchurch.org.uk*

Copyright © 2005 Catholic Bishops' Conference of England and Wales, apart from those texts herewith and otherwise acknowledged:- *The General Instruction of the Roman Missal*, copyright © 2002 the International Committee on English in the Liturgy (ICEL) in the English translation; copyright © 2005 Catholic Bishops' Conference of England and Wales, in the emendations and editorial arrangement. *Celebrating the Mass,* copyright © 2005 Catholic Bishops' Conference of England and Wales. Texts of the *Roman Missal*, copyright © 1969, 1970 the International Committee on English in the Liturgy (ICEL); *Introduction to the Lectionary*, copyright © 1969, 1983 the International Committee on English in the Liturgy (ICEL). Scripture texts taken from the *New Revised Standard Version,* copyright © 1966 Division of Christian Education of the National Council of the Churches of Christ, USA; *The Jerusalem Bible*, published and copyright 1966, 1967 and 1968 by Darton, Longman and Todd Ltd, and used by permission of the publishers; psalms from the *Grail Psalms* copyright The Grail, published by HarperCollins Publishers with permission. *Constitution on the Sacred Liturgy*, from *Documents on the Liturgy, 1963-1979, Conciliar, Papal and Curial Texts* copyright © 1982 the International Committee on English in the Liturgy (ICEL).

Introduction. 'Recently I met with….' Vincent Nichols. *Promise of Future Glory: Reflections on the Mass.* © Darton, Longman and Todd, London, 1997, (p.16-17). Gathering. 'Some years ago…' Gertrud Mueller Nelson. *To Dance with God: Family Ritual and Community Celebration.* © Paulist Press, New Jersey, USA 1986, (p. 3). Word. 'A small wood sculpture…' Hans-Ruedi Weber. *The Book that reads me: A Handbook for Bible Study Enablers.* © WCC Publications, Geneva, 1995, (p. ix). Thanksgiving. 'Always and everywhere…' Emily Besl. *Assembly* (11.4) © Notre Dame Center for Pastoral Liturgy, IN, 1985, (p. 2). Communion. 'I went to Ethiopia…' Cardinal Basil Hume, OSB. *Light in the Lord.* © Slough: St Paul Publications, 1991. Mission. Megan McKenna. *Rites of Justice: the Sacraments and Liturgy as Ethical Imperatives.* © Orbis Books, Maryknoll, New York, 1997.

ISBN 1 86082 306 8

Contents

Foreword

There is we know deep down a hope and a meaning to our lives, which does not disappoint. It is not an object or an idea, but a person. It is Jesus Christ. It is His presence, His promises and His assurance that God is with us which gives a purpose, a meaning and a destiny to each one of us and, indeed, to the whole of humanity. We are His witnesses.

The privileged place for our meeting with Christ is the Mass. It is, as the Bishops of England and Wales have taught in *One Bread One Body*, 'the source and summit of the whole Christian life. It is the vital centre of all that the Church is and does, because at its heart is the real presence of the crucified, risen and glorified Lord, continuing and making available his saving work among us.' Christ is truly present for us in those gathered in his name, in the word proclaimed, in the person and ministry of the priest, and in the most Holy Sacrament of his Body and Blood.

With Hearts and Minds will provide those taking part in the sessions with an opportunity to reflect on how the Church invites us to take part in the celebration of the Mass. It draws on the new revised *General Instruction to the Roman Missal*, as well as our own Bishops' *Celebrating the Mass*. But more than offering an opportunity to consider the teaching of the Church, it provides an opportunity to consider how we pray the Mass, and how what we experience in the Mass might be carried into our lives, helping us to become a still more authentically Eucharistic people.

Renewal in our life in the Church can take many forms. But whatever form it takes it must involve prayer, it must involve meeting together with others, in the liturgy, in the Mass, in your small groups. Beyond this it must involve sacrifice, a sacrifice of time, a sacrifice of effort but above all it must involve a desire to do what Jesus did and to participate in his suffering and in his offering for the sake of the world.

I first experienced the power of small faith sharing communities in my first two parishes, in and near Portsmouth from 1957 to 1966. Towards the end of my period in the first parish a group of people invited me to join their monthly meetings. They met together in different houses to pray, to read a passage of the Gospel and to reflect on the circumstances of their daily lives. It was my first lesson in the value of a basic Christian community. My subsequent experience confirms that such faith clusters, or communities, allows a whole mix of people - married, unmarried, young and old - to discover a new and deeper experience of faith through prayer, scripture, community and service to others.

What struck me then about the role of the Church in our culture, and what has continued with me throughout my ministry, is that our influence is most tangibly felt through the actual witness of the people of God. The authenticity and effectiveness of that witness is in turn dependent, at least in part, on our continuing to develop and mature as people of deep spirituality and holiness.

Within smaller groups, where a degree of trust and confidence becomes inherent, people are encouraged and inspired to go further and deeper on their faith journey than they might otherwise.

I commend *With Hearts and Minds* and pray that it will bear fruit that will last for the Church in England and Wales.

✠ Cardinal Cormac Murphy O'Connor

Archbishop of Westminster

President of the Bishops' Conference of England and Wales

Introduction for Group Leaders

Aim of Study Group

- To assist participants to a deeper appreciation of the nature and role of the Liturgy in the life of the Christian Community.
- To assist participants to a deeper participation in the celebration of the Liturgy.
- To assist participants to take greater responsibility for the celebration of the Liturgy in their parish

Working with small groups

We study and learn in many ways. One of the richest ways of studying and learning is to do so with others in a group. That way one is able to benefit from other people's many different perspectives on the matter in hand, the fruit of their different experiences and situations in life. When Christians work in this way they build on their existing unity as members of the Body of Christ: it offers a precious opportunity to explore things not only intellectually but at the level of faith also. Insights that might simply pass any one of us by were we studying alone, often make more of an impact when they are heard in the context of a group.

The group provides an opportunity for people of good will to come together and reflect on the materials given. These materials are mostly key texts from the Church's tradition – Scripture, teaching of the 2nd Vatican Council, contemporary teaching regarding the Liturgy. Some of them are rather densely written: it takes a little effort for some of these to 'speak' to most of us. The group provides a healthy context for considering these writings. For seeing how what they say connects with our own experience – with our hopes and fears, joys and longings concerning the life of our parish and our own role in that.

What is the Study Group going to be looking at?

How we celebrate Mass. There are six sessions in total. After a first introductory session each one will focus on a part of the Mass. This will be explored by looking both at how Mass is celebrated in our parish, and at the Church's official teaching about the celebration of Mass.

The main official text that we will be looking at is the *General Instruction of the Roman Missal* (GIRM). (Details of other documents quoted from are given below in the section **Read and Reflect** on page xiv.)

What is GIRM?

The *General Instruction* is the universal Church's official guide to the celebration of the Mass. It is much more than a collection of rubrics for the benefit of ministers. It seeks to enable the full, active and conscious participation of the whole assembly in the collective act that is the celebration of the Eucharist.

The first version of GIRM was published in 1969 as part of the Roman Missal revised after the 2nd Vatican Council. The latest revision was published in 2002 in the new 3rd edition of the (Latin) Roman Missal. It is this revision that we will be using. An official translation of GIRM has been published in advance of the rest of the Missal, because of its importance as a teaching document for the Church. An English translation of the complete Missal is presently in preparation (and is unlikely to be published before 2007).

The revised *General Instruction* amends the existing text in some details, but also adds new material often extracted from other Church documents published since 1969, for example the *Introduction to the Lectionary* and the *Ceremonial of Bishops*. The revision of GIRM was carried out by the Holy See following more than 30 years' experience of the Church's celebration of the revised Roman Rite of the Mass.

The role of the Leaders

The task of the leadership within a *With Hearts and Minds* group is not to teach but simply to assist the group to engage with the materials given. Precisely how each group does that will depend on a number of factors, particularly the people in the group, their past experiences, and present situation. There are no goals that can be pre-set for all groups, nor is it wise to try and work out an achievement target for any particular group.

It will probably be best if each group has two leaders – the first to look after matters to do with hospitality, the second to look after the session itself.

The leader of hospitality

The leader of hospitality makes sure that

- the room is prepared for the group.
- the materials for the session are ready (e.g. for the first session, **Participant's books** – unless these have been distributed beforehand). A prayer focus in the meeting room – for example a covered table, with a candle and a bible. The leader of hospitality will need to liaise with the session leader in order to know what form the prayer will take each week. There are suggestions in the Leaders' notes, but they are only suggestions…
- Tea and coffee is ready for the group (be that as people arrive, or at the end of the session).
- there is a welcome for those arriving (including any late-comers, so they can be helped quietly to slip into the group).

Although the leader of hospitality has the responsibility for ensuring all these things are in place, they do not, of course, need to do them all themselves. It will often be more appropriate to share tasks out around the group, over the weeks.

The session leader

The session leader makes sure that:

the group starts and finishes at the agreed times.
If members need to leave promptly at the agreed time they should be able to do so, without feeling that they are missing out on what they came for. Others in the group may be free to arrive early or stay to chat over tea or coffee, for example, but it should be made clear that this is 'extra' to the work of the group.

the group keeps to the timetable for each session.
As will be seen below, time has been allocated to each part of the session, according to what is judged necessary. If the timetable is not kept to then what is most likely to be squeezed out is the reflection on the practical application of the things

discussed, and the final prayer. That would be a great pity. So don't worry if all the questions aren't answered or if the discussion takes a different form to that planned. But do try to keep the over-all shape of the session intact. (It is likely that the particular challenge is that the group moves on from the Scripture reflection in good time to spend the full 30 minutes on the Read & Reflect section.)

the group keeps to the task in hand.
Leaders' notes for each session indicate the main themes of each section. The leader should not hold the group back until each detail of each theme has been exhaustively considered. This would be harmful to the working of the group. However by preparing well and noting the main themes in advance, the leader will often be able to help a group, if it finds difficulty in coming to grips with the material, by asking a supplementary question or saying something like "looking at this the other day, I wondered about…" Again, do note that the supplementary questions provided in the leader's material are only there for when it is needed. In most cases the questions in the participants' material should be quite enough.

Above all, the session leader should have a care for the healthy working of the group.
Each group is going to be different, but a few pointers to the sort of 'difficulties' that can arise might be helpful

- Often a group will contain one or two people that will sit quietly, perhaps nervous of making any direct contribution to the discussion. The leader should be aware if any one seems to be being 'left out'. Of course, such a person may not wish to say anything, but on the other hand they may simply feel nervous about speaking in a group, in which case a little gentle encouragement might be enough to help them to feel welcome and 'safe' and able to make their contribution. A leader should never force anyone else to speak, but can gently encourage them to do so.

  The materials for the sessions give the opportunity for people to make notes in response to the questions – so that the leader might ask: 'Has anyone got anything else written down?' Reading out a thought is easier for some than speaking directly, without notes.

- Often a group will contain a person who, left to their own devices will seek to dominate the group – always willing to talk, but less willing to listen. On page 'ix' there are some 'ground rules' for groups. At the first meeting ask everyone in the group whether they are happy for the group to operate according to them. If so, it should be easier, should a particular person come to dominate the group, to thank them for their contribution, and ask whether anyone else would like to say something.

- There will sometimes be someone in the group who is always ready to tell others "what the Church teaches" or, whenever a question is asked, become immediately pre-occupied with "what is the official teaching about this?" Such attitudes can get in the way of how a group is intended to work. It is not that Church teaching is unimportant, far from it. There is plenty of such teaching offered here for reading and reflection. But the group's learning is about much more than simply coming to know what the Church teaches, it is also about learning what this teaching means to us, and how it connects with our lives. No teaching can of itself help us to learn these things – we will only learn them as we listen to each other, as we reflect on what is taught and on our experience of the life of faith.

- Sometimes a group or someone in the group will come up with a question that can seem very important, but no one present knows the answer to. There is no need to panic! No group knows the answer to everything, and sometimes we can't immediately find the right answer to even the most basic sounding sorts of questions. If this happens – just acknowledge the question and ask if anyone would like to try and find out something more about it for the next meeting. If no-one else feels up to it, it is probably best if the session leader says they will take it on. (And then after the meeting contact the parish team, or someone else, who might be able to offer some help!)

Expenses

Offering refreshments incurs costs – particularly if something more than tea and coffee is involved. Decisions need to be made in advance of the first meeting about whether it is in fact possible to offer refreshments, and if so whether the proposal is that the cost will be borne by the host, the group or the parish. Please note that it is suggested that groups are invited to consider sharing a meal together after Session 5.

There are various other costs involved in running the course – particularly the materials for leaders and participants. If the parish is not able to cover all these costs from parish funds then one reasonable way of proceeding is to agree a standard contribution across all the groups to cover the cost of the materials and refreshments, and then invite people to pay this *if they can afford it*. To avoid any embarrassment to those who cannot afford to pay the charge set, envelopes might be given out at the first meeting, asking everyone to return them, either to the next meeting, or to the Parish House, enclosing whatever it is that they are able to give.

Before you begin

Little things can make a great deal of difference to how your group will work. Be sure that the group's leaders (hospitality and session) have met before the first session to agree on who is looking after what.

Material has been provided for an introductory session in the parish for all the group leaders to come together and learn about *With Hearts and Minds*. This material is available for freely downloading on the Liturgy Office website [www. liturgyoffice.org.uk/Resources].

There are six sessions in total, which are listed below, together with the part of the Mass that is the particular focus.

Table of Sessions

Session 1	**Introduction**	
Session 2	**Gathering**	Introductory Rites
Session 3	**Word**	Liturgy of the Word
Session 4	**Thanksgiving**	Liturgy of the Eucharist – Eucharistic Prayer
Session 5	**Communion**	Communion Rite
Session 6	**Mission**	Concluding Rite

The structure and timing of each session
Each session follows the same structure.

Welcome	10 minutes	
Listen to Scripture Our Experience	20 – 30 minutes	
Read & Reflect For Discussion	30 – 40 minute	
Act	5 minutes	
Prayer	15 minutes	

It is suggested that each session lasts about an hour and a half.

The timings given above are rough estimates as to how long each part will last. It does not matter if it feels time to move on from one part a little early, or if you take a little longer over another part. However, try and keep to the general timings suggested, and always try to make sure that you finish at the agreed time.

Timings

Make sure everyone knows what time the group begins and ends and where it will take place.

Reading the materials

The *With Hearts and Minds* materials are designed to be read, and they encourage people to write as a principal way of engaging with what they read. For a variety of reasons not everyone will be able to use them in this standard format. To offer further assistance to those who cannot, the scripture readings and extracts from the various Church documents have been recorded and are available from the Liturgy Office on CD and tape. (020 7901 4850, lifeworsh@cbcew.org.uk)

The recording might be given to a person unable to sight-read for their use at home, and to listen to on headphones during the group session. In some circumstances it might be thought best to play the recording for all to hear during the session.

The discussion questions have not been put on the tape. Where there is need, these should be read out to the whole group, or by the 'translator' if the person unable to sight-read is being assisted in this way.

Practicalities to be discussed at the first session

The following guidelines will help people feel confident in the group. At the first meeting read them out, and ask people whether they are willing to accept them as governing the group. They can be found on page v in the Participant's Book.

Guidelines for the group

1. Because the group provides an opportunity for those taking part to learn from one another it is very important that we try to listen to each other. If anyone finds that they are not listening for at least twice as long as they are speaking they are going to be talking too much!

2. After the various times of reflection people will be invited to share their reflections in the group. However no-one should feel pressured to share anything that they would rather not share.

3. Proper confidentiality should be maintained. What is said in the group, is for the group, and not to be spoken of elsewhere.

Refreshments and Costs

If refreshments are available for your group's meetings, and if there is a choice as to whether they are available before the meeting or after, you should ask the group to decide which they would prefer. If there is a cost for these, and for the other materials, tell the group of this, and advise them as to how money will be collected.

It is thought that many groups might like to share a simple meal together after Session 5. The possibility of this might be mentioned at the first meeting, but it may be best to avoid asking the group to make a decision, one way or the other, until Session 3, when they will have had a chance to get to know one another a little better, and also to start to gel as a group.

Beginning your first session

Leaders' Book

The material for the Sessions follows the same layout in both the Participant's and Leader's Book even down to the page numbering. In the Leader's Book however there are notes to help you lead each session. These are found in the margins alongside the participant's text.

Before you begin

- At the beginning of each Session you will find a summary page that gives an outline of the complete session. This will help you prepare.

- Read through the Session.

- Does anything particular need to be got ready beforehand?

- Look over the questions — how would you answer them?

- Does anything in particular strike you; something you have not thought of before; something you disagree with; something you want more time to think about?

- It is unlikely that your group will have the same response as you, nor is it desirable that they should, but it is important that you are familiar with the material, understand the connection between the different parts and have an overall feel for the session.

- Some of the words and phrases may be unfamiliar — at the end of the book there is a glossary.

- Prepare the presentation of the practicalities of refreshment costs and group rules.

The elements of each session

Aim

Welcome

Listen to Scripture

Our Experience

Read & Reflect

For Discussion

Act

Prayer

With Hearts and Minds

Aim

A simple aim is given at the beginning of each session.

Welcome

After some first words of welcome, you may wish to begin with a moment of silence, or by lighting a candle. If you wish to begin with a prayer, one of the following would be suitable.

> God our Father,
> your Son promised to be with all who gather in his name.
> Make us aware of his presence among us
> and fill us with his grace, mercy and peace,
> so that we may live in truth and love.
>
> We ask this through our Lord Jesus Christ, your Son,
> who lives and reigns with you in the unity of the Holy Spirit,
> one God for ever and ever.

Prayer for Pastoral or Spiritual Meetings

> Be close to this gathering,
> Lord God of steadfast truth.
> Grant us patience in listening,
> wisdom in speaking,
> and courage to do the works of the gospel.
>
> We ask this through our Lord Jesus Christ, your Son,
> who lives and reigns with you in the unity of the Holy Spirit,
> one God for ever and ever.

Prayer for Pastoral or Spiritual Gatherings

Session One: Don't presume that everyone in the group knows everyone else. One way of making introductions, of course, is simply to ask everyone to introduce themselves. Maybe a better way (particularly in a group where you know a good number of those present do not know others in the group) is to ask everyone to speak to the person next to them, learn their name, and something about them, and then for each in these pairs to introduce the other to the larger group. (One particular benefit of doing this, is that it means when you start everyone will already have spoken in the group, and to the group – in a relatively unthreatening fashion – before the session properly gets under way. This can help overcome any initial reticence about speaking in a group.)

From **Session Two** onwards be sure to give some time in which people can share their experience of the previous week's 'Act' (see below).

Listen to Scripture

Each session includes the reading of scripture. The scripture reading for each week is printed in the participants' material, mostly using the NRSV translation. Some participants might prefer to use another translation, such as the Jerusalem Bible translation used in the Sunday or weekday lectionary, or another translation they may use in their regular prayer or Bible reading. There is no reason for everyone to use the same translation, and there are many advantages in encouraging people to bring their own bible to use at the meetings.

The following is a tried and tested method of proclaiming the scripture, listening to it and reflecting on what has been heard. It follows the principles of 'lectionary based catechesis'. It is a method very often used to assist adults in their learning of the faith.

1. Have the reading read aloud. (It may be helpful to choose readers the week before so that they can prepare.) Invite the other members of the group to listen without reading the text for themselves.

2. Allow a significant silence after the reading for people to take it to heart and ponder on it (about 3 minutes).

3. Have the reading read again (either by the same reader or, perhaps better, by a second reader).

4. After the second time invite each person to share what has struck them from the reading: a word, a phrase, a sentence; perhaps an image, perhaps a question. Maybe not everyone will say something, but allow time for people to mull over what they hear before moving on.

Our experience

This section helps those taking part to start to explore the session's main theme.

Sometimes the questions asked in this section will link quite directly to the scripture reading. At other times they will not. However they will always be opening up things that will be explored in the Read & Reflect section.

'Ordinary' people's experience is too often neglected as a resource for the community's learning about the ways of faith. However it is a rich resource, giving a context to the questions being explored, putting flesh on the bones of the 'theory' and sometimes challenging the truth of the 'theory', helping us to find new ways of expressing the unchanging core truths of our faith.

Questions for all are included. When you are preparing the session you may wish to consider what your own answers to the questions would be. In the session it may be helpful to invite people to write down their responses first.

In the side column of this book are listed some likely responses. Don't think of this as a checklist of correct answers or even an exhaustive list of possible answers.

Some may appear 'incorrect' but it is important that people engage honestly with the questions and it is good to be prepared for these too. Listen out to see which ones are voiced by people in your group; if some are not, you might want to invite people to consider some of them. In Session 1: **Our Experience** asking, for example: 'Do you think the main reason that some people come to Mass is to set a good example for their children?'

There are also supplementary questions given which might be useful to 'keep the conversation going' or develop the discussion. But often it may be more appropriate to move the discussion on to the next participant's question or next section.

Read & Reflect

The documentation is drawn from three primary sources.

> **CSL**   *Constitution on the Sacred Liturgy* (Sacrosanctum Concilium) – which is the document from the 2nd Vatican Council which called on the Church to deepen her understanding of the liturgy, and in particular to work for the full, active and conscious participation of all the faithful in the Church's worship.

> **GIRM**   *General Instruction of the Roman Missal* – which is the official guide to the celebration of Mass prepared for the Roman Catholic Church throughout the world. A revised version of GIRM was published in 2002 in the new 3rd edition of the (Latin) Roman Missal. The official translation of GIRM has been published in advance of the rest of the Missal, because of its importance as a teaching document for the Church. An English translation of the complete Missal is presently in preparation, perhaps to be published in 2007.

> **CTM**   *Celebrating the Mass* – which is a pastoral guide to the celebration of Mass prepared by the Bishops of England and Wales and addressing the particular situation and needs of the Church in their dioceses. It is intended to assist people in their understanding of the Liturgy of the Mass, and to be a companion to GIRM.

The *General Instruction* and *Celebrating the Mass* are published by Catholic Truth Society.

Enabling reflection

With each of the elements of the sessions it is important to allow time for reflection, not just a first hearing, but for pondering on what has been heard.

Sometimes, as with the scripture reflection, there is a rather formal process suggested. At other times simply allow a little time and space.

You may wish to have the texts read aloud with a pause between each one. It may also be helpful to encourage people to look over the material before the meeting, so that they come already somewhat familiar with it. The participants' booklets give space for them to write down first reflections in response to questions – again, helping people to think for themselves before opening things up to the group as a whole. Do be aware that not all participants may be confident reading. (See *Reading the materials* page ix.)

For Discussion

The notes on **Our Experience** on page xiii apply.

Further reading

At the end of each session supplementary texts are provided. They are principally there for people to take home and read at another time. They often give the complete text of a passage which has been quoted only in part in Read & Reflect, as well as offering some additional perspectives.

Act

Thinking about the things of faith is good. Putting them into practice is better. In each of the sessions some practical steps are suggested by which those taking part can make the things discussed more securely part of their lives, for example when they next go to Mass.

Keeping a Journal

It is also suggested that those taking part are likely to benefit from keeping a journal. Although this might sound something unusual and unlikely, it can be very helpful.

Over a series of meetings all sorts of things can come up – new insights, feelings. Unless we take a moment to note them down, they are often quickly forgotten, and an opportunity for deeper learning is lost. All that is necessary is to write down just a few thoughts and observations, after each meeting, or practical exercise, and perhaps also after Mass each Sunday. Simply noting what has struck us and, perhaps, how we feel about it.

Because these are private notes there is no need to worry about whether we are putting things in the 'right words'… these are just notes to help us call to mind what we thought at the time and might otherwise forget. A personal review of a journal before each meeting is a good way of preparing for the meeting. Reviewing the journal at the end of the series of meetings is almost certain to reveal what a rich process of reflection we have been part of.

It is important for the leader to emphasise that what is written in each journal remains private to the person concerned, and that it is a matter entirely for that person whether they choose to share it with others, or not. At no point in the process are those taking part going to be asked to share with others what is in their journal. This should be made clear to all at the first meeting.

A note about Journals is also provided in the Participant's book page v.

Prayer

Each session ends with a time of prayer.

It should be based on the simple structure of:

- Gather
- Listen
- Respond
- Send forth

For each session a number of ideas are given under each of these headings.

The 'Gather' and 'Send forth' elements could be the same each week.

Elements which are particularly appropriate are shown in **bold type**.

What is important is that the group spends time praying together. So if the suggestions given for particular music, readings or actions do not really seem to suit your group, then feel free to adapt them as necessary. However it is suggested that in adapting what is offered, you try to link the prayer, actions, texts and songs with the topics being considered, in the same way we have tried to do.

Sometimes, though hopefully not often, the prayer may need to be curtailed because the time has over run. It may be best then: to pause for silent prayer, pray the Lord's Prayer together and say the Blessing.

The person preparing the prayer will need to liaise with the leader of hospitality, so that the prayer focus for each session also suits the nature and content of the time of prayer. Where a bible forms part of the prayer focus it would be good to use it for the scripture passage in the time of prayer.

Before you begin

Read through the session.

Look over the questions — how would you answer them?

Does anything in particular strike you; something you have not thought of before; something you disagree with; something you want more time to think about.

It is unlikely that your group will have the same response as you nor it is desirable that they should but it is important that you are familiar with the material, understand the connection between the different parts and have an overall feel for the session.

Aim

How we participate in the life of Christ through the celebration of the Mass.

Welcome

Listen to Scripture

Matthew 14: 13–21

The crowd are drawn to Jesus who are fed from what they themselves provide.

Our Experience

- Why do I come to Sunday Mass?
- What do I bring to Sunday Mass that in Christ might become food for all?

Read & Reflect

Two paragraphs from the Second Vatican Council's Constitution on the Sacred Liturgy — Sacrosanctum Concilium *that speak of the centrality of liturgy to the life of the Church and the desire of the Church that all the faithful be led to full, conscious, and active participation in liturgical celebrations. The extracts from the* General Instruction *reiterate this desire.*

For Discussion

- 'Participation… of the sort which is desired by the Church and demanded by the very nature of the celebration' (GIRM 18).
  Describe a celebration of Mass that fully engaged you?
  What was different for you?

- 'That… leads to a conscious, active, and full participation of the faithful both in body and in mind, a participation burning with faith, hope, and charity' (GIRM 18)
  In what ways do we take part in the Mass?

- '…to which the Christian people have a right and duty by reason of their Baptism' (GIRM 18)
  What do I expect of the Church and Mass?
  What does the Church and Mass expect of me?

Act

Introduction to Journals.
In preparation for next Sunday's Mass.
In preparation for the next meeting.

Prayer

1. Introduction

How we participate in the life of Christ through the celebration of the Mass.

Recently I met with a group of people preparing to be received into the Catholic Church. I asked if they would be willing to share their reasons for taking this step. They were very ready indeed! One woman spoke of her experience at Sunday Mass, which she had attended with her husband and family for many years. She spoke of how she had always felt 'taken up' and 'included' in what was going on. I asked if she was speaking about the singing, the preaching, or the 'sense of community'? To my surprise she rejected these alternatives and said that it was 'what went on at the altar' that had always touched her deeply, and she felt taken up in that.

This woman, I believe, sensed the deeper reality of the Church. She was able to experience something of that communion of life which lies beyond many of its more outward expressions. She had a sensitivity to those realities which came through to her as an invitation, a call, to a fuller life. She was responding to that experience by seeking formally and consciously the full communion of life in the Catholic Church.

✠ In the name of the Father
and of the Son
and of the Holy Spirit.

Welcome

See section in Leader's Introduction. pg. xii.

Listen to Scripture

This section helps those taking part to start to explore the session's main theme.

After the reading of the passage invite people to share a word or phrase that struck them. The questions may not at first appear always to refer to the scripture but they begin to open up the theme of the session and connect it with people's lives.

Questions for all are printed on the participant's sheets. Below are listed some likely responses. Don't think of this as a checklist of correct answers or even an exhaustive list of possible answers. Some may appear 'incorrect' but it is important that people engage honestly with the questions. Listen out to see which ones are voiced by people in your group; if some are not you might want to invite people to consider some of them. For example, asking: 'Do you think the main reason that some people come to Mass is to set a good example for their children'.

There are also given below supplementary questions which might be useful to 'keep the conversation going' or develop the discussion though it will often be better to move on to the next question or section.

Listen to Scripture

Now when Jesus heard
the news of John the Baptist's death,
he withdrew from there in a boat
to a deserted place by himself.
But when the crowds heard it,
they followed him on foot from the towns.
When he went ashore, he saw a great crowd;
and he had compassion for them and cured their sick.

When it was evening, the disciples came to him and said,
"This is a deserted place, and the hour is now late;
send the crowds away
so that they may go into the villages
and buy food for themselves."

Jesus said to them,
"They need not go away; you give them something to eat."

They replied,
"We have nothing here but five loaves and two fish."

And he said, "Bring them here to me."
Then he ordered the crowds to sit down on the grass.
Taking the five loaves and the two fish,
he looked up to heaven,
and blessed and broke the loaves,
and gave them to the disciples,
and the disciples gave them to the crowds.
And all ate and were filled;
and they took up what was left over of the broken pieces,
twelve baskets full.
And those who ate were about five thousand men,
besides women and children.

Matthew 14: 13–21

Our Experience

- Why do I come to Sunday Mass?
- What do I bring to Sunday Mass that in Christ might become food for all?

....

....

....

....

....

....

....

....

....

....

....

....

....

....

....

....

....

Why do I come to Sunday Mass?

Issues that may arise from the first question — people will often have a mixture of reasons:

- Obligation
- To be community
- To meet people
- To make space each week for God
- Time out from routine
- Time for prayer
- To set an example to my children
- To be challenged afresh
- To give thanks
- To be a minister

Possible supplementary questions:

- If there was no obligation would you come? What would draw you?

What do I bring to Sunday Mass that might in Christ become food for all?

Possible responses

- Myself
- My talents, gifts
- My experience of life
- My last week
- Joys and sorrows, hopes for the future
- Care for other people, for children

Possible supplementary questions:

- What can help us recognise what each person brings to the celebration?
- What can help us to share these gifts?
- What does it cost to share these gifts?

Read & Reflect

**Describe a celebration of Mass that fully engaged you.
What was different for you?**

Possible responses

- A joyful celebration — lots of people involved.
- Good music
- A homily that spoke to me
- A prayerful Mass
- A Mass that responded to an event/crisis
- A wedding or a funeral
- I felt different at the end of it.

Possible supplementary questions:

- Is there a difference between 'lots of people being involved' and 'my being involved'?
- Is there a difference between 'music I like' and 'music that draws me closer to Christ'?

In what ways do we take part in the Mass?

Possible responses

- Gathering
- Praying
- Listening to scripture
- Making responses
- Intercessions
- Singing
- Posture
- Communion

Possible supplementary questions:

- Do we ever think of how we use our bodies in prayer? Sometimes, for example, we pray without using any words — we genuflect, kneel or make the sign of the cross.
- Is there a difference between when we pray together and when we pray alone?

Read & Reflect

CONSTITUTION ON THE SACRED LITURGY

10. The liturgy is the summit toward which the activity of the Church is directed; at the same time it is the font from which all the Church's power flows. For the aim and object of apostolic works is that all who are made children of God by faith and baptism should come together to praise God in the midst of his Church, to take part in the sacrifice, and to eat the Lord's supper.

14. The Church earnestly desires that all the faithful be led to that full, conscious, and active participation in liturgical celebrations called for by the very nature of the liturgy. Such participation by the Christian people as "a chosen race, a royal priesthood, a holy nation, God's own people" (1 Pet 2:9; see 2: 4–5) is their right and duty by reason of their baptism.

In the reform and promotion of the liturgy, this full and active participation by all the people is the aim to be considered before all else. For it is the primary and indispensable source from which the faithful are to derive the true Christian spirit and therefore pastors must zealously strive in all their pastoral work to achieve such participation by means of the necessary instruction.

GENERAL INSTRUCTION OF THE ROMAN MISSAL

17. It is therefore of the greatest importance that the celebration of the Mass — that is, the Lord's Supper — be so arranged that the sacred ministers and the faithful taking part in it, according to the proper state of each, may derive from it more abundantly those fruits for the sake of which Christ the Lord instituted the Eucharistic Sacrifice of his Body and Blood and entrusted it to the Church, his beloved Bride, as the memorial of his Passion and Resurrection.

18. This will best be accomplished if, with due regard for the nature and the particular circumstances of each liturgical assembly, the entire celebration is planned in such a way that it leads to a conscious, active, and full participation of the faithful both in body and in mind, a participation burning with faith, hope, and charity, of the sort which is desired by the Church and demanded by the very nature of the celebration, and to which the Christian people have a right and duty by reason of their Baptism.

For Discussion

- *'Participation... of the sort which is desired by the Church and demanded by the very nature of the celebration'* (Girm 18).
  Describe a celebration of Mass that fully engaged you.
  What was different for you?

- *'That... leads to a conscious, active, and full participation of the faithful both in body and in mind, a participation burning with faith, hope, and charity'* (Girm 18)
  In what ways do we take part in the Mass?

- *' ...to which the Christian people have a right and duty by reason of their Baptism'* (Girm 18)
  What do I expect of the Church and Mass?
  What does the Church and Mass expect of me?

....

....

....

....

....

....

....

....

....

....

....

....

**What do I expect of the Church and Mass?
What does the Church and Mass expect of me?**

Possible responses

- To give me a time of quiet – to help me get my bearing

- To know what is right

- To be there for me

- To forgive my sins

- Hatch, match and dispatch

- To show us we belong together

- To help us remember the place of God in our lives

- A place to go pray

- To be there on Sundays

- To bring my children to Mass

- To love my neighbour

- To pay for the upkeep of the parish

Possible supplementary questions:

- People often complain that people are eager to take their rights but not to carry out their responsibilities. What are the rights of the baptised? What are their responsibilities?

- What difference has seeing adults baptised at the Easter Vigil made to your appreciation of being baptised?

Act

See section in Introduction (page xv)

Act

- *Beginning your Journal. See page v.*

- *In preparation for next Sunday's Mass.*
  What has happened during this week?
  What is most on my mind today?
  Remember and reflect on these things on Sunday in your time of preparation before the beginning of Mass.

- *In preparation for the next meeting.*
  What at Mass made an impression on you?
  In what ways did last Sunday's Mass suggest how we might live as Christ in the world.

Prayer

"This is my commandment,
that you love one another as I have loved you.
No one has greater love than this,
to lay down one's life for one's friends.
 You are my friends if you do what I command you.
I do not call you servants any longer,
because the servant does not know what the master is
doing;
but I have called you friends,
because I have made known to you
everything that I have heard from my Father.
 You did not choose me but I chose you.
And I appointed you to go and bear fruit, fruit that will last,
so that the Father will give you
whatever you ask him in my name.
I am giving you these commands
so that you may love one another.

John 15: 12-17

Our Father, who art in heaven,
hallowed be thy name.
Thy kingdom come.
Thy will be done on earth, as it is in heaven.
Give us this day our daily bread,
and forgive us our trespasses,
as we forgive those who trespass against us,
and lead us not into temptation,
but deliver us from evil.

Prayer

See section in Introduction (page xvi)

Gather

- Light a candle(s) and/or time of silence:
  In the name of the Father…
  Let us begin our time of prayer with a few moments silence.

- Sing a song or chant about the Church, Sunday, Praise of God, or Baptism (for example the refrain *We come to share our story* or *Ubi Caritas* (Taizé)).

Listen

- John 15: 12–17

Respond

- Time of silent reflection

- Invite people to name concerns for prayer. Don't forget to include the group itself and its forthcoming time together.

- **The Lord's Prayer**
  All say the Lord's Prayer together.
  Consider standing up and/or adopting the 'orans' position.
  Introduce in these or similar words:
  Let us now pray in the words our Saviour gave us: or
  Following our Lord's teaching, let us say with faith and trust:

Sending Forth

- Leader:
  The Lord bless us, and keep us from all evil,
  and bring us to everlasting life.

  All: *Amen*

Further Reading

- At the end of session material is provided for further reading. This includes the complete text of those passages which have been quoted only in part as well as offering other related paragraphs.

CONSTITUTION ON THE SACRED LITURGY

106. By a tradition handed down from the apostles which took its origin from the very day of Christ's resurrection, the Church celebrates the paschal mystery every eighth day; with good reason this, then, bears the name of the Lord's day or Sunday. For on this day Christ's faithful are bound to come together into one place so that; by hearing the word of God and taking part in the eucharist, they may call to mind the passion, the resurrection and the glorification of the Lord Jesus, and may thank God who "has begotten them again, through the resurrection of Jesus Christ from the dead, unto a living hope" (1 Pet. 1:3). Hence the Lord's day is the original feast day, and it should be proposed to the piety of the faithful and taught to them so that it may become in fact a day of joy and of freedom from work. Other celebrations, unless they be truly of greatest importance, shall not have precedence over the Sunday which is the foundation and kernel of the whole liturgical year.

GENERAL INSTRUCTION OF THE ROMAN MISSAL

27. At Mass — that is, the Lord's Supper — the People of God is called together, with a priest presiding and acting in the person of Christ, to celebrate the memorial of the Lord, the Eucharistic Sacrifice. For this reason Christ's promise applies in an outstanding way to such a local gathering of the holy Church: 'Where two or three are gathered in my name, there am I in their midst' (Mt 18:20). For in the celebration of Mass, in which the Sacrifice of the Cross is perpetuated, Christ is really present in the very liturgical assembly gathered in his name, in the person of the minister, in his word, and indeed substantially and continuously under the Eucharistic species.

28. The Mass is made up, as it were, of two parts: the Liturgy of the Word and the Liturgy of the Eucharist. These, however, are so closely interconnected that they form but one single act of worship. For in the Mass the table both of God's word and of Christ's Body is prepared, from which the faithful may be instructed and refreshed. There are also certain rites that open and conclude the celebration.

Celebrating the Mass

21. The celebration of Mass is the action of Christ and the Church, which is "the Sacrament of unity", namely the holy people of God united and ordered under the Bishop. It is the action in which the Christian people, 'a chosen race, a royal priesthood, a holy nation, a people set apart', expresses its unity and its nature. It is the action of the whole people of God, ministers and congregation, united with Christ, who is head of the Body.

    Within the one body of Christ there are many gifts and responsibilities. But just as each organ and limb is necessary for the sound functioning of the body (see 1 Corinthians 12), so every member of the assembly has a part to play in the action of the whole. It is therefore of the greatest importance that in all circumstances and on every occasion the celebration be so organised that priest, ministers, and faithful may all take their own part. The participation of all is demanded by the nature of the liturgy, and, for the faithful, is their right and duty by reason of their baptism.

    - By apostolic tradition, the Church gathers on the Lord's Day to celebrate the Lord's Supper. This Sunday Eucharist, at which the entire local community assembles and in which all play their proper parts, is the primary manifestation of the local Church and, as such, the most important and normative form of Eucharistic celebration. It should be in every sense inclusive and not be needlessly multiplied. (Although more than one mass will often be celebrated in a parish on a Sunday a balance needs to be kept between what is convenient, and what helps the Church to become an authentic community of faith and mission and celebrate the Liturgy fully, richly and reverently.) The celebration of other Sacraments, when the Roman Ritual allows, may be accommodated within it.

    - In the celebration of the Eucharist, all present, ordained or lay faithful, render the particular service corresponding to their role and function in the assembly. A celebration is the work of the whole body of Christ; the ministers and other members of the assembly have a part in the action and have a contribution to make. Each of these special services is performed for the good of the whole and for the glory of God.

Before you begin

Read through the session.

Look over the questions — how would you answer them?

Does anything in particular strike you; something you have not thought of before; something you disagree with; something you want more time to think about.

It is unlikely that your group will have the same response as you nor it is desirable that they should but it is important that you are familiar with the material, understand the connection between the different parts and have an overall feel for the session.

Aim

What the assembly is and how it is called to be.

Welcome

Listen to Scripture

1 Peter 2: 4–10

You are a chosen race, a royal priesthood, a consecrated nation, a people set apart to sing the praises of God.

Our Experience

• What does it mean to be a parish?

• In what ways are we a parish community?

• Are there any called by God who would not feel 'at home' in our church?

Read & Reflect

The extracts from the General Instruction *and* Celebrating the Mass *make reference to the reading from the First Letter of Peter. The assembly — those who gather to celebrate Mass, priest and people — are 'a chosen race…' In the Introductory Rites the assembly is formed into a community ready to listen to God's word and to celebrate the Eucharist worthily.*

For Discussion

• What does it mean to have been made 'God's own' (cf. GIRM 95), a people 'called together in Christ' (cf. CTM 5)?

• As a group describe what happens between the beginning of Mass and the first reading and why we might do these things?

• What are the ways we express our unity in common prayer?

Act

Reminder about journals.
When going to Mass next Sunday
Before Mass begins

Prayer

2. Gathering

Some years ago, I spent an afternoon caught up in a piece of sewing I was doing. The waste basket near my sewing machine was filled with scraps of fabric cut away from my project. This basket of discards was a fascination to my daughter, Annika, who at the time was not yet four years old. She rooted through the scraps searching out the long bright strips, collected them to herself, and went off. When I took a moment to check on her, I tracked her whereabouts to the back garden where I found her sitting in the grass with a long pole she had gotten from the garage. She was fixing the scraps to the top of the pole with great sticky wads of tape. Mothers sometimes ask foolish questions, and I asked one. I asked her what she was doing. Without taking her eyes from her work she said, "I'm making a banner for a procession. I need a procession so that God will come down and dance with us." With that, she solemnly lifted her banner to flutter in the wind, and slowly she began to dance.

The Lord be with you.
And also with you.

Welcome

Before beginning the session you may want to give people a few minutes to talk about the ways in which they prepared for last Sunday's Mass and spent time afterwards reflecting on it.

Help people to notice what was good about this not just to say what they did.

Listen to Scripture

This section helps those taking part to start to explore the session's main theme.

See notes on page xiii.

What does it mean to be a parish?

Possible responses

- Shared identity
- Common experience
- Sense of tradition
- To be part of a community of communities.
- To know that we are called to be Christ in this place.
- The way we individuals connect with the wider Church

Possible supplementary questions:

- What difference does it make knowing that we are one of many parishes in our diocese?

Listen to Scripture

Come to him, a living stone,
    though rejected by mortals
    yet chosen and precious in God's sight,
and like living stones,
let yourselves be built into a spiritual house,
to be a holy priesthood,
to offer spiritual sacrifices acceptable to God
through Jesus Christ.

For it stands in scripture:
"See, I am laying in Zion
a stone, a cornerstone chosen and precious;
and whoever believes in him will not be put to shame."
To you then who believe, he is precious;
but for those who do not believe,
"The stone that the builders rejected
has become the very head of the corner,"
and "A stone that makes them stumble,
and a rock that makes them fall."
They stumble because they disobey the word,
as they were destined to do.
But you are a chosen race, a royal priesthood,
a holy nation, God's own people,
in order that you may proclaim the mighty acts of him
who called you out of darkness into his marvellous light.
Once you were not a people,
but now you are God's people;
once you had not received mercy,
but now you have received mercy.

1 Peter 2: 4–10

Our Experience

- What does it mean to be a parish?

- In what ways are we a parish community?

- Are there any called by God who would not feel 'at home' in our church?

....

....

....

....

....

....

....

....

....

....

....

....

....

....

....

....

....

....

....

In what ways are we a parish community?

Possible responses
- We gather on Sundays
- We all have a parish priest
- Social Club
- School
- SVP and other organisations
- Of this place
- Parish Council

Possible supplementary questions:
- Does it appear for some people in the group parish is formed by place or building and for other people parish is about relationships?

Are there any called by God who would not feel 'at home' in our church?

What seems to be a question about others turns about to be a question about ourselves and who we see ourselves to be.

Possible responses
- Sinners
- The self-righteous
- People with no faith in God
- People of other faiths
- Young people
- Other Christians
- The divorced and remarried
- Refugees
- Victims of abuse

Possible supplementary questions:

Taking one or two of these groups, ask what makes them feel not at home here.
- Should our parish communities always be comfortable places?
- In what ways do we feel united with people of Christian communities, and other faiths etc.?

What does it mean to have been made 'God's own' (cf. GIRM 95), a people 'called together in Christ' (cf. CTM 5)?

Possible responses

- To be special
- To have a reason for life
- To be grateful
- I was Anglican and felt called to be Catholic
- To identify with others
- To be the Church
- I was not chosen I was born Catholic
- I do not feel worthy to be called

Possible supplementary questions:

- What are we called together for?
- How does this happen?

Read & Reflect

GENERAL INSTRUCTION OF THE ROMAN MISSAL

95. In the celebration of Mass the faithful form a holy people, a people whom God has made his own, a royal priesthood, so that they may give thanks to God and offer the spotless Victim not only through the hands of the priest but also together with him, and so that they may learn to offer themselves. They should, moreover, endeavour to make this clear by their deep religious sense and their charity toward brothers and sisters who participate with them in the same celebration.

    Thus, they are to shun any appearance of individualism or division, keeping before their eyes that they have only one Father in heaven and accordingly are all brothers and sisters to each other.

96. Indeed, they form one body, whether by hearing the word of God, or by joining in the prayers and the singing, or above all by the common offering of Sacrifice and by a common partaking at the Lord's table. This unity is beautifully apparent from the gestures and postures observed in common by the faithful.

97. The faithful, moreover, should not refuse to serve the People of God gladly whenever they are asked to perform some particular ministry or role in the celebration.

CELEBRATING THE MASS

22. Christ is always present in the Church, particularly in its liturgical celebrations. In the celebration of Mass, which is a memorial of the Sacrifice of the cross, Christ is really present first of all in the assembly itself: "Where two or three come together in my name, there am I in their midst" (Matthew 18:20). At Mass "the faithful form a holy people, a people whom God has made his own, a royal priesthood, so that they may give thanks to God and offer the spotless Victim not only through the hands of the priest but also together with him, and so that they may learn to offer themselves. They should, moreover, endeavour to make this clear by their deep religious sense and their charity toward brothers and sisters who participate with them in the same celebration."

139. In the Introductory Rites, Christ joins the Church to himself and gathers her children to join their voices to his perfect hymn of praise. Thus, the liturgical assembly, "where two or three come together in Christ's name, and where he is found in their midst (cf. Mt 18:20), is the 'first image that the Church gives of herself'". Indeed the assembly itself is also the first instance of Christ's presence in the liturgy.

    The purpose of the Introductory Rites is to ensure that the faithful, who come together as one, establish communion and dispose themselves to listen properly to God's word and to celebrate the Eucharist worthily.

For Discussion

- What does it mean to have been made 'God's own' (cf. GIRM 95), a people 'called together in Christ' (cf. CTM 5)?

- As a group describe what happens between the beginning of Mass and the first reading and why we might do these things.

- What are the ways we express our unity in common prayer?

....

....

....

....

....

....

....

....

....

....

....

....

....

....

As a group describe what happens between the beginning of Mass and the first reading and why we might do these things.

Possible responses

- Entrance procession/song
- Greeting
- Introduction to the Mass
- Penitential Rite — different forms
- Blessing and Sprinkling of Water
- Gloria
- Opening Prayer or Collect

Possible supplementary questions:

- Who is involved in each action?
- What does each part say about the people who gather? e.g. Gloria — a people called to sing God's praise.

What are the ways we express our unity in common prayer?

Possible responses

- We come together on Sundays
- Through song, silence, prayer
- We do the same things at the same time — standing, sitting, kneeling, singing
- By serving one another
- By taking collections
- In offering food for the hungry

Possible supplementary questions:

- It may be useful to recall from the first session 'the ways we take part in the Mass'
- Is there a difference between praying together and praying alone?

Act

_____

Act

- *When going to Mass next Sunday choose one of the following to do:*
  Notice the ways in which people arrive at the church: in groups, singly, what forms of transport?
  Is there space for people to meet and greet?
  Do they make use of it?

  Is there anything to indicate this a welcoming community?
  Would someone of impaired mobility need help to enter the church?

  What else is going on in the neighbourhood?
  What sort of witness is this to the wider community?

- *Before Mass begins choose one of the following to do:*
  Be aware of the people gathering at Mass with you.

  Notice their diversity: the young, the old, families and single people, people of different races and cultures etc.
  Notice the different ways that people prepare themselves for Mass.
  Notice what other things are taking place in preparation for Mass.

  Consider the various circumstances that have brought us together at this place at this time for our common celebration.

Prayer
See section in Introduction (page xvi)

Gather

- Light a candle(s) and/or time of silence:
  In the name of the Father...
  Let us begin our time of prayer with a few moments silence.

- Sing a song or chant about Gathering, the Church in heaven and on earth, Praise of God, or Jesus (for example *All are welcome* or *Laudate omnes gentes* (Taizé)).

Prayer

Like the deer that yearns
for running streams,
so my soul is yearning
for you, my God.

My soul is thirsting for God,
the God of my life;
when can I enter and see
the face of God?

These things will I remember
as I pour out my soul:
how I would lead the rejoicing crowd
into the house of God,
amid cries of gladness and thanksgiving,
the throng wild with joy.

Why are you cast down, my soul
why groan within me?
Hope in God; I will praise yet again,
my saviour and my God.

O send forth your light and your truth;
let these be my guide.
Let them bring me to your holy mountain
to the place where you dwell.

And I will come to the altar of God,
the God of my joy.
My redeemer, I will thank you on the harp,
O God, my God.

Psalms 41: 2–3. 5–6; 42: 3–4

Listen

- Psalms 41: 2–3. 5–6; 42: 3–4

Respond

- Time of silent reflection
- **Pray for some of the groups of people who came up in the discussion.**
- End the prayer with either:

Confirm, O God,
in unity and truth
the Church you gather in Christ.
Encourage the fervent,
enlighten the doubtful,
and bring back the wayward.
Bind us together in mutual love,
that our prayer in Christ's name
may be pleasing to you.

Grant this through our Lord
Jesus Christ, your Son,
who lives and reigns with you
in the unity of the Holy Spirit,
God for ever and ever.
Amen.

- Or all say the Lord's Prayer together.
  Consider standing up and/or adopting the 'orans' position.
  Introduce in these or similar words:
  Let us now pray in the words our Saviour gave us: or
  Following our Lord's teaching, let us say with faith and trust:

Sending Forth

- Leader:
  *The Lord bless us,
  and keep us from all evil,
  and bring us to everlasting life.*
  All: *Amen*

Further Reading

CONSTITUTION ON THE SACRED LITURGY

7. To accomplish so great a work, Christ is always present in his Church, especially in its liturgical celebrations. He is present in the sacrifice of the Mass, not only in the person of the minister, "the same now offering, through the ministry of priests, who formerly offered himself on the cross," but especially under the eucharistic elements. By his power he is present in his sacraments, so that when a man baptises it is really Christ himself who baptises. He is present in his word, since it is he himself who speaks when the holy Scriptures are read in the Church. He is present, lastly, when the Church prays and sings, for he promised: "Where two or three are gathered together in my name, there I am in the midst of them" (Mt 18:20).

GENERAL INSTRUCTION OF THE ROMAN MISSAL

A. The Introductory Rites

46. The rites preceding the Liturgy of the Word, namely the Entrance, Greeting, Penitential Act, *Kyrie*, *Gloria*, and Collect, have the character of a beginning, introduction, and preparation.

    Their purpose is to ensure that the faithful, who come together as one, establish communion and dispose themselves to listen properly to God's word and to celebrate the Eucharist worthily.

    In certain celebrations that are combined with Mass according to the norms of the liturgical books, the Introductory Rites are omitted or performed in a particular way.

The Entrance

47. After the people have gathered, the Entrance chant begins as the priest enters with the deacon and ministers. The purpose of this chant is to open the celebration, foster the unity of those who have been gathered, introduce their thoughts to the mystery of the liturgical season or festivity, and accompany the procession of the priest and ministers.

CELEBRATING THE MASS

Assembly

22. Christ is always present in the Church, particularly in its liturgical celebrations. In the celebration of Mass, which is a memorial of the Sacrifice of the cross, Christ is really present first of all in the assembly itself: "Where two or three come together in my name, there am I in their midst" (Matthew 18:20). At Mass "the faithful form a holy people, a people whom God has made his own, a royal priesthood, so that they may give thanks to God and offer the spotless Victim not only through the hands of the priest

but also together with him, and so that they may learn to offer themselves. They should, moreover, endeavour to make this clear by their deep religious sense and their charity toward brothers and sisters who participate with them in the same celebration."

23. The liturgical assembly is never a random group of individuals but the gathering of God's people to exercise its royal priesthood in the sacrifice of praise. Everything in the celebration is organised to encourage and foster an awareness of this assembly's common dignity and purpose, mutual interdependence, and connectedness with the wider Church.

24. The Church earnestly desire that all the faithful be led to that full, conscious, and active participation in liturgical celebrations called for by the very nature of the liturgy. Such participation by the Christian people as 'a chosen race, a royal priesthood, a holy nation, God's own people' (1 Pt 2: 9; see 2:45) is their right and duty by reason of their baptism.

- In the celebration of the Eucharist the assembly is united in and by the principal actions of gathering, listening to God's word, praying for life of the Church and the world, giving thanks, sharing communion and being sent out for the work of loving and serving God.

- Times for silent reflection allow the assembly to engage more deeply in the mystery being celebrated.

- The dialogues between the assembly and its ministers, and the acclamations have a special value as signs of communal action and as means of effective communication. More importantly yet they foster and bring about communion between priest and people.

- Singing is one of the most potent of all expressions of communal awareness and common purpose.

- Uniformity in posture and gesture likewise expresses and fosters a unity of spirit and purpose.

Before you begin

Read through the session.

Look over the questions — how would you answer them?

Does anything in particular strike you; something you have not thought of before; something you disagree with; something you want more time to think about.

It is unlikely that your group will have the same response as you nor it is desirable that they should but it is important that you are familiar with the material, understand the connection between the different parts and have an overall feel for the session.

Aim

Christ continues to speak through his word and in Christ we listen & respond.

Welcome

Listen to Scripture

Luke 4: 13–21

Jesus teaches in the synagogue in his home town and tells those who have gathered: 'This text is being fulfilled today even as you listen.'

Our Experience

- How is this passage from scripture Good News today?
- How do I experience Christ present in the proclamation of the word?

Read & Reflect

Extracts from the General Instruction *and* Celebrating the Mass. *The first paragraph explains the importance of silence; the remainder the structure and purpose of the Liturgy of the Word. 'All must listen with reverence to the readings of God's word: meditating on the word, taking it to heart, and beginning to respond to it in prayer.' (CTM 51)*

For Discussion

- What qualities should be looked for in one who proclaims the word?
- What qualities should be looked for in one who listens to the word?
- In what ways does our community respond to the word proclaimed?

Act

Prepare for Sunday's Mass by reading the gospel and other readings.

On the days after Sunday return to the Gospel or other readings, continuing to reflect on them.

Prayer

3. Word

A small wood sculpture by an unknown Tanzanian artist stands on my desk. It shows a woman holding a bible in her hands, holding it high above her head. As one looks at the tattooed face of this African woman, it seems that a big smile is just beginning to break through. Is she going to reveal a great secret which gives her deep joy?

The artist has captured the climax of a story told in East Africa. A village woman used to walk around always carrying her Bible. "Why always the Bible?" her neighbours asked teasingly. "There are so many other books you could read." The woman knelt down, held the Bible high above her head and said, "Yes, of course there are many books which I could read. But there is only one book which reads me."

This is the word of the Lord.
Thanks be to God.

Welcome

Before beginning the session you may want to give people a few minutes to talk about what the group noticed about the time of preparation before Mass both inside and outside the church.

Help people to notice what was good about this not just to say what they saw.

Listen to Scripture

This section helps those taking part to start to explore the session's main theme.

See notes on page xiii.

Listen to Scripture

Jesus, filled with the power of the Spirit,
returned to Galilee,
and a report about him spread through all
the surrounding country.
He began to teach in their synagogues
and was praised by everyone.

When he came to Nazareth,
where he had been brought up,
he went to the synagogue on the sabbath day,
as was his custom.
He stood up to read,
and the scroll of the prophet Isaiah was given to him.
He unrolled the scroll
and found the place where it was written:
"The Spirit of the Lord is upon me,
because he has anointed me
to bring good news to the poor.
He has sent me to proclaim release to the captives
and recovery of sight to the blind,
to let the oppressed go free,
to proclaim the year of the Lord's favour."

And he rolled up the scroll,
gave it back to the attendant, and sat down.
The eyes of all in the synagogue were fixed on him.
Then he began to say to them,
"Today this scripture has been fulfilled in your hearing."

Luke 4: 14–21

Our Experience

- How is this passage from scripture Good News today?

- How do I experience Christ present in the proclamation of the word?
(cf. CsL 7, Further reading from Session 2 page 18)

....

....

....

....

....

....

....

....

....

....

....

....

....

....

....

....

....

....

....

....

How is this passage from scripture Good News today?

Possible responses

- It still has a message for us
- The oppressed still need to be set free
- It gives reasons for hope
- Christ's message is for all time

Possible supplementary questions:

- What other passages of scripture are Good News for us?

How do I experience Christ present in the proclamation of the word?
(cf. CsL7, Further reading from Session 2 page 18)

Possible responses

- As encouragement and challenge
- I am reminded of his life and what he did for us
- In the faith of the reader

Possible supplementary questions:

- How do we show respect for Christ present in the word?

What qualities should be looked for in one who proclaims the word?

Possible responses

- Clear voice
- Good communicator
- Understanding of text
- Believing what they proclaim
- Reflective person
- Ability to tell a story
- Presence
- Ability to engage
- Commitment to prepare for ministry

Possible supplementary questions:

- If you had to prioritise these qualities, what order would you put them in?

Read & Reflect

GENERAL INSTRUCTION OF THE ROMAN MISSAL

The Liturgy of the Word

29. When the Sacred Scriptures are read in the Church, God himself speaks to his people, and Christ, present in his own word, proclaims the Gospel...

Silence

56. The Liturgy of the Word is to be celebrated in such a way as to promote meditation, and so any sort of haste that hinders recollection must clearly be avoided. During the Liturgy of the Word, it is also appropriate to include brief periods of silence, accommodated to the gathered assembly, in which, at the prompting of the Holy Spirit, the word of God may be grasped by the heart and a response through prayer may be prepared. It may be appropriate to observe such periods of silence, for example, before the Liturgy of the Word itself begins, after the First and Second Reading, and lastly at the conclusion of the Homily.

CELEBRATING THE MASS

153. The readings from Sacred Scripture and the chants between the readings form the main part of the Liturgy of the Word. The Homily, Profession of Faith, and Prayer of the Faithful expand and complete this part of the Mass. For in the readings God speaks with his people, opening up to them the mystery of redemption and salvation, and nourishing their spirit; Christ himself is present in the midst of the faithful through his word. The Homily is an integral part of the liturgy to assist the assembly to hear the voice of the Lord in his word. By their silent listening and pondering, and by their singing and acclamation, the people make God's word their own, and they also affirm their acceptance of it by the Profession of Faith. Finally, having been nourished by this word, the assembly makes petition in the Prayer of the Faithful, praying for the needs of the entire Church and for the salvation of the whole world.

155. The proper celebration of the Liturgy of the Word involves many elements and several ministers, but care is necessary so that the many human words and elements do not obscure the divine word itself.

For Discussion

- What qualities should be looked for in one who proclaims the word?

- What qualities should be looked for in one who listens to the word?

- In what ways does our community respond to the word proclaimed?

....

....

....

....

....

....

....

....

....

....

....

....

....

....

....

....

....

What qualities should be looked for in one who listens to the word?

Possible responses

- Attentiveness
- Concentration
- Able to make good use of silence
- Reflectiveness
- Desire to understand
- Ability to apply what is heard to life

Possible supplementary questions:

- How can we develop these qualities?
- Does someone who proclaims need first to listen?

In what ways does our community respond to the word proclaimed?

Possible responses

- Homily
- Profession of Faith
- Prayer
- SVP
- Parish projects
- CAFOD and other appeals
- Sharing faith with others: children; catechesis; family; non-believers.
- In our work
- In all the ways we live

Possible supplementary questions:

- What might we do in response to last week's Gospel?

Act

Act

- Prepare for Sunday's Mass by reading the gospel and other readings

- On the days after Sunday return to the Gospel or other readings, continuing to reflect on them.

You may wish to continue this practice over the coming weeks.

Prayer

See section in Introduction (page xvi).

Gather

- Light a candle(s) and/or time of silence:
  *In the name of the Father…
  Let us begin our time of prayer
  with a few moments silence.*

- Enthrone a Bible or Lectionary

- Sing a song or chant about Jesus, the Word, or a Gospel Acclamation (Alleluia):
  (Oh the word of my Lord
  – refrain, Litany of the Word)

Listen

- Repeat part of the opening scripture.

- **John 6: 60–69**
  The words I have spoken to you are spirit and they are life.

Prayer

When many of his disciples heard Jesus' teaching,
they said, "This teaching is difficult; who can accept it?"

But Jesus, being aware that his disciples
were complaining about it,
said to them, "Does this offend you?
Then what if you were to see the Son of Man
ascending to where he was before?
It is the spirit that gives life; the flesh is useless.
The words that I have spoken to you are spirit and life.
But among you there are some who do not believe."

For Jesus knew from the first
who were the ones that did not believe,
and who was the one that would betray him.
And he said, "For this reason I have told you
that no one can come to me
unless it is granted by the Father."

Because of this many of his disciples turned back
and no longer went about with him.

So Jesus asked the twelve,
"Do you also wish to go away?"
Simon Peter answered him,
"Lord, to whom can we go?
You have the words of eternal life.
We have come to believe
and know that you are the Holy One of God."

John 6: 60–69

Respond

- The reader says '*This is the word of the Lord*' and passes the bible (which has been read from) to the next person who kisses the book. They then say '*This is the word of the Lord*' and pass it on in a similar manner.
- Time of silent reflection
- Prepared simple **Intercessions** praying for Church, World, etc.

For the Church
throughout the world;
that it may always proclaim the good news:

> *Pause for silent prayer*
> Lord, in your mercy.
> **Hear our prayer.**

For leaders and those in authority:
that they may be open to Christ's message of peace:

> *Pause for silent prayer*
> Lord, in your mercy.
> **Hear our prayer.**

For all who minister the word in our community
may they be faithful to the Gospel:

> *Pause for silent prayer*
> Lord, in your mercy.
> **Hear our prayer.**

For all those in need;
may they be comforted by Christ's healing word:

> *Pause for silent prayer*
> Lord, in your mercy.
> **Hear our prayer.**

Sending Forth

- Leader:
  The Lord bless us,
  and keep us from all evil,
  and bring us to everlasting life.
  All: Amen

In preparation

It is suggested that as part of Session 5: Communion there is a meal or sharing of food. Discuss with the group if they would like do this and how it might happen.

Further Reading

LECTIONARY FOR MASS: INTRODUCTION

10.   The Church has honoured the word of God and the Eucharistic mystery with the same reverence, although not with the same worship, and has always and everywhere intended and endorsed such honour. Moved by the example of its Founder, the Church has never ceased to celebrate his paschal mystery by coming together to read 'in all the Scriptures the things written about him' (Lk 24:27) and to carry out the work of salvation through the celebration of the memorial of the Lord and through the sacraments. 'The preaching of the word is necessary for the sacramental ministry. For the sacraments are sacraments of faith and faith has its origin and sustenance in the word.'

The Church is nourished spiritually at the table of God's word and at the table of the Eucharist: from the one it grows in wisdom and from the other in holiness. In the word of God the divine covenant is announced; in the Eucharist the new and everlasting covenant is renewed. The spoken word of God brings to mind the history of salvation; the Eucharist embodies it in the sacramental signs of the Liturgy.

It can never be forgotten, therefore, that the divine word read and proclaimed by the Church in the Liturgy has as its one goal the sacrifice of the New Covenant and the banquet of grace, that is, the Eucharist. The celebration of Mass in which the word is heard and the Eucharist is offered and received forms but one single act of divine worship. That act offers the sacrifice of praise to God and makes available to God's creatures the fullness of redemption.

GENERAL INSTRUCTION OF THE ROMAN MISSAL

Reading and Explaining the Word of God

29.   When the Sacred Scriptures are read in the Church, God himself speaks to his people, and Christ, present in his own word, proclaims the Gospel.

Therefore, all must listen with reverence to the readings from God's word, for they make up an element of greatest importance in the Liturgy. Although in the readings from Sacred Scripture God's word is addressed to all people of every era and is understandable to them, nevertheless, a fuller understanding and a greater effectiveness of the word is fostered by a living commentary on the word, that is, the Homily, as part of the liturgical action.

B. The Liturgy of the Word

55.   The main part of the Liturgy of the Word is made up of the readings from Sacred Scripture together with the chants occurring

between them. The Homily, Profession of Faith, and Prayer of the Faithful, however, develop and conclude this part of the Mass. For in the readings, as explained by the Homily, God speaks to his people, opening up to them the mystery of redemption and salvation, and offering them spiritual nourishment; and Christ himself is present in the midst of the faithful through his word. By their silence and singing the people make God's word their own, and they also affirm their adherence to it by means of the Profession of Faith. Finally, having been nourished by it, they pour out their petitions in the Prayer of the Faithful for the needs of the entire Church and for the salvation of the whole world.

The Biblical Readings

57. In the readings, the table of God's word is prepared for the faithful, and the riches of the Bible are opened to them. Hence, it is preferable to maintain the arrangement of the biblical readings, by which light is shed on the unity of both Testaments and of salvation history. Moreover, it is unlawful to substitute other, non-biblical texts for the readings and responsorial Psalm, which contain the word of God.

60. The reading of the Gospel is the high point of the Liturgy of the Word. The Liturgy itself teaches that great reverence is to be shown to it by setting it off from the other readings with special marks of honour: whether on the part of the minister appointed to proclaim it, who prepares himself by a blessing or prayer; or on the part of the faithful, who stand as they listen to it being read and through their acclamations acknowledge and confess Christ present and speaking to them; or by the very marks of reverence that are given to the *Book of the Gospels*.

The Homily

65. The Homily is part of the Liturgy and is strongly recommended, for it is necessary for the nurturing of the Christian life. It should be an exposition of some aspect of the readings from Sacred Scripture or of another text from the Ordinary or from the Proper of the Mass of the day and should take into account both the mystery being celebrated and the particular needs of the listeners.

The Prayer of the Faithful

69. In the Prayer of the Faithful, the people respond in a certain way to the word of God which they have welcomed in faith and, exercising the office of their baptismal priesthood, offer prayers to God for the salvation of all. It is fitting that such a prayer be included, as a rule, in Masses celebrated with a congregation,

so that petitions will be offered for the holy Church, for civil authorities, for those weighed down by various needs, for all men and women, and for the salvation of the whole world.

CELEBRATING THE MASS

Sacred Scripture

69. Pre-eminent among the texts of the Mass are the biblical readings with their accompanying scriptural chants, for even now from the word of God handed down in writing God speaks to the people, "and it is from the continued use of Sacred Scripture that the people of God, docile to the Holy Spirit under the light of faith, receive the power to be Christ's living witnesses before the world."

70. All must listen with reverence to the readings of God's word: meditating on the word, taking it to heart, and beginning to respond to it in prayer.

Liturgy of the Word

151. The Mass is made up of the Liturgy of the Word and the Liturgy of the Eucharist, which are so closely connected as to form one act of worship. In the word of God the divine covenant is announced; in the Eucharist the new and everlasting covenant is embodied and renewed.

152. The chosen people entered into a special covenant with God at Sinai, a covenant that was renewed and fulfilled on Calvary. By hearing the word proclaimed in worship, the faithful again enter into the unending dialogue between God and the covenant people, a dialogue sealed in the sharing of the Eucharistic food and drink. The meaning of Communion is proclaimed in the word; the message of Scripture is made actual once again in the Communion banquet. The proclamation of the word is thus integral to the Mass and at its very heart.

154. The *Lectionary for Mass*, revised at the direction of the Second Vatican Council, has opened up the treasures of the Bible, so that richer fare might be provided for the faithful at the table of God's word. The *Introduction to the Lectionary* speaks extensively of the place of the word of God in the plan of salvation and in the life of the Church. All who share in the ministry of the word will want to study this introduction and take its teaching to heart.

155. The proper celebration of the Liturgy of the Word involves many elements and several ministers, but care is necessary so that the many human words and elements do not obscure the divine word itself.

Silence

91. Silence is an important element in all communication. It is particularly important to allow for silence as a part of the dialogue between God and the community of faith. It allows for the voice of the Holy Spirit to be heard in the hearts of the people of God and to enable them to unite personal prayer more closely with the word of God and the public voice of the Church. During liturgical silence all respond in their own way, recollecting themselves, pondering what has been heard, petitioning and praising God in their inmost spirit.

92. Liturgical silence is not merely an absence of words, a pause, or an interlude. It is a stillness, a quieting of spirits, a making of time and leisure to hear, assimilate, and respond. Any haste that hinders reflectiveness should be avoided. The dialogue between God and the community of faith taking place through the Holy Spirit requires intervals of silence, suited to the assembly, so that all can take to heart the word of God and respond to it in prayer.

   • Liturgical silence is a corporate activity shared in by all present, by which all support and sustain each other in profound prayerful solidarity. It demands a stillness and prayerful concentration, which the priest celebrant and all ministers can help to bring about.

   • Structurally, liturgical silence is indispensable to the rhythm of a balanced celebration. Without periods of prayerful and reflective silence the celebration can become perfunctory in its haste or burdensome in its unrelieved sound and song.

   • The purpose of any particular silence, depends on where it occurs in each part of the celebration. In the Penitential Act, all pause to remember their sinfulness and the loving-kindness of God in Christ. At the opening prayer, they put themselves and their deepest needs and desires before God. After the readings and Homily, they savour God's word, ponder it in their hearts like Mary (see Luke 2:19), and apply it to their lives. After Communion, they praise and pray to God in their hearts.

   • Even before the celebration itself, calm and opportunities for silent prayer and reflection have their proper place in the church, in the sacristy and in adjacent areas so that those gathering for the assembly of the Church may recollect themselves and begin to prepare for prayer together. Providing opportunities for such calm and quiet is one of the many ways in which a community is able to show hospitality to those gathering for worship.

Reader

41. In proclaiming the word of God from Sacred Scripture, readers exercise their responsibility in mediating the presence of Christ. God speaks to the assembly through them, and the impact of God's message will depend significantly on their conviction, their preparation, and their delivery.

42. The richness in the quantity and in the variety of readings in the *Lectionary* challenges those who are called upon to proclaim the Scriptures at Mass. Each of the individual sacred authors reflected on the meaning of God's action in history from their own perspective. They employed various literary forms to convey the message of salvation, ranging, for example, from narratives and the poetry of the psalms to prophetic oracles and parables, from theological expositions to apocalyptic visions. A reader will proclaim the word of the Lord more fully and more effectively if he or she has an awareness of the literary form of a particular reading or psalm.

   • Both to assist the assembly to appreciate the genre and context of the different passages of Scripture and benefit from a different voice, it is better to have a different reader for each reading.

   • The responsorial psalm should be sung by a psalmist or cantor, but, if necessary, may be led by a reader.

   • When there is no deacon, a reader may carry the *Book of the Gospels* before the presiding priest in the entrance procession and lay it on the altar.

   • When there is no deacon, the reader may, from the ambo, announce the intentions in the General Intercessions.

Psalmist

43. …The psalmist has the special task of drawing the assembly into the proclamation of the word of God in the psalm or other biblical canticle that comes between the readings by introducing the psalm responses and Gospel acclamation to the assembly, and by singing the verses of the responsorial psalm and Gospel Acclamation verses. The psalmist may also introduce the antiphons to the assembly and sing the verses of the psalms used. The psalmist should have the ability to sing, and an aptitude for correct pronunciation and diction.

Homily

71. Although in the readings from Sacred Scripture God's word is addressed to all people of every era and is understandable to them, nevertheless, a fuller understanding and a greater effectiveness of the word is fostered by a living commentary on the word, that is, the Homily, as part of the liturgical action.

Before you begin

Read through the session.

Look over the questions — how would you answer them?

Does anything in particular strike you; something you have not thought of before; something you disagree with; something you want more time to think about.

It is unlikely that your group will have the same response as you nor it is desirable that they should but it is important that you are familiar with the material, understand the connection between the different parts and have an overall feel for the session.

Aim

How we participate in Christ's sacrifice of praise.

Welcome

Listen to Scripture

Psalm 145

Psalms 144–150 are known collectively as the 'Hallel' or praise psalms. In them God is thanked for what he has done. My soul give praise to the Lord… It is God who gives bread to the hungry.

Our Experience

- What am I thankful for?
- To whom do I give thanks?

Read & Reflect

The extracts from Celebrating the Mass *introduce the Eucharistic Prayer as the centre and summit of the entire celebration and then give a commentary on the movement and shape of prayer.*

For Discussion

- How would I describe the Eucharistic Prayer?
- How do I participate in the Eucharistic Prayer?
- How are we joined to Christ in offering his sacrifice to the Father?
  (cf. CTM 186)

Act

Listen to the Eucharistic Prayer at Sunday Mass, and afterwards note any words or phrases in the Eucharistic Prayer (including its Preface and acclamations) and reflect on any that particularly strike you.

Use these in your prayer over the coming days.

Prayer

4. Thanksgiving

How we participate in Christ's sacrifice of praise.

Always and everywhere.

Not just here and now
gathered with this assembly
offering this prayer
but at all times and in all places
we give you thanks.

Because you first loved us
with profound simplicity
we know that
in the tasks we accomplish
the responsibilities we undertake
our manner of speaking
or attentive listening
our patience with frustrations
and generous hospitality
you see our thanks
all summed up
manifested
expressed
in this prayer of praise.

May all that we do
always and everywhere
give you thanks.

Let us give thanks to the Lord our God.
It is right to give him thanks and praise.

With Hearts and Minds

Welcome

Give time for people to speak about how they responded to the Word last Sunday.

Notice the variety of responses.

Listen to Scripture

This section helps those taking part to start to explore the session's main theme.

See notes on page xiii.

Listen to Scripture

Alleluia!
My soul give praise to the Lord;
I will praise the Lord all my days,
make music to my God while I live.

Put no trust in the powerful,
mere mortals in whom there is no help.
Take their breath, they return to clay
and their plans that day come to nothing.

They are happy who are helped by Jacob's God,
whose hope is in the Lord their God,
who alone made heaven and earth,
the seas and all they contain.

It is the Lord who keeps faith for ever,
who is just to those who are oppressed.
It is God who gives bread to the hungry,
the Lord, who sets prisoners free.

The Lord who gives sight to the blind,
who raises up those who are bowed down,
the Lord, who protects the stranger
and upholds the widow and orphan.

It is the Lord who loves the just
but thwarts the path of the wicked.
The Lord will reign for ever,
Zion's God, from age to age.

Psalm 145

Our Experience

- What am I thankful for?
- To whom do I give thanks?

....

....

....

....

....

....

....

....

....

....

....

....

....

....

....

....

....

....

What am I thankful for?

Possible responses
- Family
- Friends
- Life
- Grandchildren
- Health
- Wealth
- A kind deed

Possible supplementary questions:
- Is there a difference between being pleased/content and giving thanks?
- What is necessary to feel thankful?

_____

To whom do I give thanks?

Possible responses
- God
- My family
- Those who have shaped me
- Those who work for peace

Possible supplementary questions:
- Why do we give thanks?

Read & Reflect

How would I describe the Eucharistic Prayer?

Possible responses

- Long
- It is when the host becomes Jesus
- It is remembering what we give thanks for
- It is about the consecration
- We remember those who have died/Mass Intentions
- There are different prayers
- When we pray for the pope and the bishop
- Waves of spoken text

Possible supplementary questions:

- Why is the Eucharistic Prayer the centre and summit of the celebration?

Read & Reflect

CELEBRATING THE MASS

186. The Eucharistic Prayer, the centre and summit of the entire celebration, sums up what it means for the Church to celebrate the Eucharist. It is a memorial proclamation of praise and thanksgiving for God's work of salvation, a proclamation in which the Body and Blood of Christ are made present by the power of the Holy Spirit and the people are joined to Christ in offering his Sacrifice to the Father. The Eucharistic Prayer is proclaimed by the priest celebrant in the name of Christ and on behalf of the whole assembly, which professes its faith and gives its assent through dialogue, acclamations, and the Amen. Since the Eucharistic Prayer is the summit of the Mass, it is appropriate for its solemn nature and importance to be enhanced by being sung.

187. The Eucharistic Prayer is proclaimed over the people's gifts. Through this prayer which has a rich and varied tradition, the Church gives praise and thanks for God's holiness and justice and for all God's mighty deeds in creating and redeeming the human race, deeds which reached their climax in the incarnation, life, death, and resurrection of Jesus Christ. In the Eucharistic Prayer the mystery of Christ's saving death and resurrection is recalled; the Last Supper is recounted; the memorial Sacrifice of his Body and Blood is presented to the Father; and the Holy Spirit is invoked to sanctify the gifts and transform those who partake of them into the body of Christ, uniting the assembly and the whole Church and family of God, living and dead, into one communion of love, service, and praise to the glory of the Father.

For Discussion

- How would I describe the Eucharistic Prayer?

- How do I participate in the Eucharistic Prayer?

- How are we joined to Christ in offering his sacrifice to the Father? (cf. CTM 186)

....

....

....

....

....

....

....

....

....

....

....

....

....

....

....

....

....

How do I participate in the Eucharistic Prayer?

Possible responses

- silent attentiveness

- singing acclamations

- giving thanks

- posture

- joining myself with the words of the Prayer as it is prayed by the priest.

Possible supplementary questions:

- What helps/hinders my taking a full part in the prayer?

How are we joined to Christ in offering his sacrifice to the Father? (cf. CTM 186)

Possible responses

- Uniting my life with his

- Uniting my prayer with his

- Allowing myself to be loved by Christ

- Participating in Mass

- In being a loving parent

- Saying and living the Great Amen

Possible supplementary questions:

- What is the cost of being united with Christ?

Act

Act

- Listen to the Eucharistic Prayer at Sunday Mass, and afterwards note any words or phrases in the Eucharistic Prayer (including its Preface and acclamations) and reflect on any that particularly strike you.

- Use these in your prayer over the coming days.

Prayer

My soul glorifies the Lord,
my spirit rejoices in God, my Saviour.
He looks on his servant in her lowliness;
henceforth all ages will call me blessed.

The Almighty works marvels for me.
Holy his name!
His mercy is from age to age,
on those who fear him.

He puts forth his arm in strength
and scatters the proud-hearted.
He casts the mighty from their thrones
and raises the lowly.

He fills the starving with good things,
sends the rich away empty.

He protects Israel, his servant,
remembering his mercy,
the mercy promised to our fathers,
to Abraham and his sons for ever

Glory be to the Father, and to the Son,
and to the Holy Spirit.
As it was in the beginning, is now, and ever shall be
world without end. Amen.

Magnificat
Luke 1: 46–55

Prayer

*See section in Introduction
(page xvi)*

Gather

- Light a candle(s) and/or time
  of silence:
  In the name of the Father…
  Let us begin our time of
  prayer with a few moments
  silence.

- Sing a song or chant about
  thanksgiving, praise of God, a
  Memorial Acclamation

Listen

- **Magnificat** (Luke 1: 46–55)
  perhaps antiphonally

Respond

- Time of silent reflection

- People are invited, after a time
  of reflection, to say **what
  they are thankful for**, after
  each one sing or say a short
  phrase such as a Great Amen
  or Glory to God.

Sending Forth

- Leader:
  *The Lord bless us,
  and keep us from all evil,
  and bring us to everlasting life.*
  All: Amen

For next week

*If there is a meal or sharing of
food as part of next week's session
check that people will have time
for it.*

Further Reading

Eucharistic Prayer

189. The following elements may be recognised as characteristic of the Eucharistic Prayer. They do not all appear with equal weight in every Eucharistic Prayer.

Dialogue

190. Since the celebration of Mass is a communal action, the dialogue between priest celebrant and the assembly is of special value. It is not only an external sign of communal celebration, but also fosters and brings about communion between priest and people. The dialogue establishes at the outset that the Eucharistic Prayer is prayed in the person and power of the Lord who is with the Church, and in the name of the whole assembly and indeed of the whole Church in heaven and on earth. All are invited, in the biblical term, to lift up their hearts, that is, to raise up and place in God's presence their entire being, thoughts, memories, emotions, and expectations, in grateful attention and anticipation.

- The voice, gestures, and stance, the entire demeanour of the priest celebrant help to convey the importance and the urgency of this invitation. This may be most effectively achieved by singing.

- Before the dialogue, the priest may introduce the Eucharistic Prayer by suggesting very briefly particular motives for thanksgiving.

Preface

191. The praise and thanksgiving from which the entire Eucharist takes its name is especially concentrated in the "preface", which proclaims the Church's thanks for the saving work of God. In the Eastern tradition this is a fixed part of the Eucharistic Prayer, beginning the praise of God and the rehearsal of God's mighty deeds that continue throughout the prayer. In the Roman tradition the preface has been a variable element, stressing one aspect of God's saving work according to the day, the feast, the season, or the occasion. In the current English edition over eighty such prefaces from ancient and more recent sources are provided for use with Eucharistic Prayers I, II, and III.

- The preface is not a preliminary to the Eucharistic Prayer, but the first part of it. It indicates a proclamation, a speaking out before God and the faithful, rather than a foreword or prelude. For this reason it is most appropriately sung.

- The Eucharistic Prayer is always expressed in the first person plural. It is the whole assembly of the faithful that joins itself to Christ in acknowledging the great things God has done and in offering the Sacrifice, even when one voice speaks in the name of all. It is the responsibility of the priest, acting in the person of Christ, the head of the Church, to proclaim the prayer with and for the people, to engage their attention, and to elicit their involvement throughout.

- Eucharistic Prayer II has a proper preface, based like the rest of the prayer on an ancient Roman model, but other prefaces may be substituted for it, especially those which summarise the mystery of salvation, such as the Common Prefaces.

- Eucharistic Prayer IV is constructed on an Eastern model. Its preface is a fixed and integral part of the prayer, whose themes continue beyond the *Sanctus*. For this reason, it is always to be used with its own preface. This is also true of the four forms of the Eucharistic Prayer for Various Needs and Occasions, and the Eucharistic Prayers for Masses with Children.

SANCTUS ACCLAMATION

192. In this acclamation the assembly joins its voice to that of all creation in giving glory to God, with words inspired by the vision of Isaiah (6:3). In each celebration of the Eucharist , the Church is taken up into the eternal liturgy in which the entire communion of saints, the heavenly powers, and all of creation give praise to the God of the universe.

- This acclamation is an integral part of the Eucharistic Prayer. It belongs to priest and people together. Of its very nature it is a song and should be sung, even if on occasion the preface is not sung. Choir or cantor parts may also be sung if they facilitate and enhance the congregation's participation.

- Settings of the Sanctus Acclamation, together with Memorial Acclamation and Amen should form a unity which reflects the unity of the whole Eucharistic Prayer.

Epiclesis

193. In these sections of the prayer, before and after the narrative of institution, the Church invokes God's Spirit to hallow and consecrate the gifts, asking that they become the Body and Blood of Christ, and to gather those who receive them into a true communion of faith and love. Through the sanctifying power of the Holy Spirit the repetition of the Lord's words of institution is efficacious, the memorial of Christ's death and resurrection is

effected, and the Church is built up again as the body of Christ in the world.

- The life-giving power of the Spirit, who moved over the waters in the first days of creation and overshadowed Mary in the moment of the incarnation, is vividly expressed by the ancient gesture of bringing together the hands with the palms downward and extended over the elements to be consecrated. When done with great gravity and deliberation, this gesture can reinforce powerfully the understanding of the words and of the Spirit's action. This is a laying on of hands and is the same sacramental gesture used in Ordination, Confirmation, the Anointing of the Sick, and the Sacrament of Reconciliation.

- In accord with ancient tradition, if there are concelebrating priests, they stretch out both their hands toward the elements. The gesture made by the concelebrants should not be exaggerated, drawing attention to the action of the concelebrants. The full impact of their gesture is best conveyed when the concelebrants simply and naturally accompany the gestures of the presider.

Institution Narrative and Consecration

194. At the heart of the Eucharistic Prayer, the account of the Last Supper is recited. The words of Jesus, in which he gave himself to his disciples as their food and drink, are now repeated in the context of this prayer of praise. In the power of the Spirit, these words achieve what they promise and express: the presence of Christ and his Sacrifice among his people assembled. Everything for which God has been thanked and praised, all that was accomplished in the history of salvation, is summed up and made present in the person of the crucified and risen Lord.

- This narrative is an integral part of the one continuous prayer of thanksgiving and blessing. It should be proclaimed in a manner which does not separate it from its context of praise and thanksgiving.

- As a narrative it is also recited for the benefit of the assembly. It should therefore be proclaimed reverently, audibly, and intelligibly.

- On concluding the words over the bread, the priest shows the Body of the Lord to the people, and subsequently does the same with the chalice. The scale of the gesture will be indicated by the size and situation of the assembly. The gesture should be deliberate and reverent, but not prolonged, for this would affect the unity and continuity of the Eucharistic Prayer. It is most desirable that this gesture of 'showing' be quite distinct from the elevation, which forms part of doxology of the prayer.

- The bread must not be broken during the institution narrative. The Eucharistic Prayer is not a dramatic presentation of the Lord's Supper but a thanksgiving prayer offered in remembrance of that event and the other saving events of the Paschal Mystery. It is about anamnesis not mimesis. The bread that has become the Body of the Lord is not broken until the fraction rite, the Breaking of the Bread.

Memorial Acclamation

195. The Memorial Acclamation of the people in the Eucharistic Prayer confesses the Church's belief in the central mystery of our faith, the Paschal Mystery of Christ's death, resurrection, and presence among his people.

- The Memorial Acclamations provided are not specific to any Eucharistic Prayers; each may be used with any of the prayers.
- As acclamations they are intended to be sung.
- The memorial acclamation should not be replaced by other texts.

Anamnesis and Offering

196. The whole action of the Eucharist is done in obedience to the Lord's command, as a memorial of him, recalling especially his blessed Passion, glorious Resurrection, and Ascension into heaven. The Church understands this memorial as a living representation before God of the saving deeds which God has accomplished in Christ, so that their fullness and power may be effective here and now. In this memorial representation, the Church offers the one Sacrifice of praise and thanksgiving, a sacramental offering of the Sacrifice made "once for all" by Christ, the "holy and living Sacrifice" that "brings salvation to all the world." It is an offering made by the whole Church, but especially by those here and now assembled who, in the power of the Holy Spirit, offer themselves with and through Christ, the Victim and Priest who joins the Church's offering to his own.

Intercessions

197. By the grace of the Holy Spirit, the Church has become a single offering in Christ to the glory of God the Father. It now prays that the fruits of this Sacrifice may be experienced throughout the Church and the world. (In Eucharistic Prayer I, the intercessions are divided, some before, some after the

institution narrative.) The Blessed Virgin Mary and the Saints are named as the prime examples of the fruits of this redemptive Sacrifice and as forerunners in the communion of the living and the dead. Praying in communion with Mary and the other saints of God, the assembly now intercedes for the living and the dead in union with the Lord, who for ever lives to make intercession (see Hebrews 7:25).

- Local patrons or saints whose Feast or memory is being celebrated may be mentioned in the intercessions of Eucharistic Prayer III.

Doxology

198. Faithful to the Jewish pattern of prayer known and used by Jesus and his disciples, the Eucharistic Prayer concludes where it began, with an ascription of praise and glory to God, which is endorsed and ratified by all present in their acclamation *Amen*. Saint Paul considered this ratification by the assembly to be essential to the thanksgiving prayer (see 1 Corinthians 14:15-16), and early Christian writers laid great stress on it as the people's confirmation of all that was proclaimed on their behalf by the priest.

199. Through Christ, with him, and in him, all is turned to the Father's glory by the action of the Holy Spirit. At this climax of the prayer the consecrated elements are raised high in a gesture that vividly expresses the true nature of the Eucharistic Sacrifice as the offering of the Church through Christ the High Priest, with Christ, who is really present in the Church, in Christ, who has incorporated his people into himself by the action of the Holy Spirit.

- The Doxology is part of the Eucharistic Prayer rather than an acclamation. As such it is proper to the prayer spoken or sung by the priest alone. The lay faithful participate in this prayer in faith and silence, and then through their acclamation, the Great Amen.

- The profound importance of the assembly's ratification and acclamation can be difficult to bring out in the one short word *Amen*. It should be sung or at the very least spoken loudly both at the Sunday and weekday celebrations. Musical settings which prolong the *Amen* or repeat it can all help the assembly to experience and express its true power.

- At the conclusion of the Eucharistic Prayer, the priest should make a distinct pause to make clear that the Eucharistic Prayer (the 'giving thanks') is complete and that the Communion Rite (the 'breaking and sharing') is about to begin.

5. Communion

Before you begin

Read through the session.

Look over the questions — how would you answer them?

Does anything in particular strike you; something you have not thought of before; something you disagree with; something you want more time to think about.

It is unlikely that your group will have the same response as you nor it is desirable that they should but it is important that you are familiar with the material, understand the connection between the different parts and have an overall feel for the session.

Aim

Our sharing in the gifts of Christ's Body and Blood deepens us in communion.

Welcome

Listen to Scripture

Luke 24: 13–35

The story of the journey to Emmaus is often seen as following the structure of Mass: Christ first breaks open the scripture and then he took bread, blessed and broke it, and gave it to them. We are told the disciples recognised Christ in the breaking of bread and this phrase is used in the Acts of Apostles to refer to the Mass.

Our Experience
- What is it like to share your story with someone?
- What is it like to share a meal with someone?

Read & Reflect

The extracts from the General Instruction *suggest that the greater integrity of the sign of communion the greater our participation in communion.*

For Discussion
- How does the Breaking of Bread reveal Christ?
- In what ways do we express unity with Christ and with each other in the Communion Rite?
- What helps/hinders our celebration of Communion?

Act

See whether your journal notes on the Sunday scriptures help you to recognise Christ's presence in your daily living.

Where have you had the opportunity to be Christ for others?

Prayer

5. Communion

Our sharing in the gifts of Christ's Body and Blood
deepens us in communion.

I went to Ethiopia when the famine was at its height. I went because I felt somebody should go from our country, just to be there...

One day I was asked to visit a settlement where people were awaiting the arrival of food which was unlikely to come. A Russian military helicopter had been put at my disposal. We had difficulty finding the place but when we landed and I got out, a small boy came up to me and took my hand. He was aged about nine or ten and had nothing on but a loin cloth. The whole of the time I spent there, that child would not let go of my hand. He had two gestures: with one hand he pointed to his mouth to indicate his need for food; the other was a strange gesture, he took my hand and rubbed it on his cheek.

I realized slowly that he was lost and totally alone and starving. I have never forgotten that incident and to this day wonder whether that child is alive. I remember when I boarded the helicopter to leave he stood and looked at me reproachfully; an abandoned, starving ten-year-old child.

I appreciated in quite a new way those two profound and fundamental needs - for food and for love. With one gesture he showed his need for food, and with the other his need for love. It was much later that day that I realized in a new way the secret of the Eucharist, for the Eucharist is food and love. Taught by that small boy, I saw what the heart of the Eucharist is – his Body and his Blood. For indeed there is no life without food, and no life worth living without love. They are two fundamental requisites for you and me. When he Jesus said he wanted us to have life and have it more abundantly, then he must give us his love, and the love he gives is pre-eminently through that sign of his love, the Eucharist.

We approach him in a sense empty-handed, for we have nothing of our own which is not his gift and we approach very often lost and in need. Conscious of our failures, conscious of not having loved enough, empty-handed and lost, we go to him and ask that he might give us his love and he says: 'Here is my Body, here is my Blood, eat and drink.' A voice speaks to us constantly: 'Come to me all you who labour and are burdened and I will refresh you. If you are hungry for the things of God, and if you are lost and in need of love, come to me and I will refresh you.' That invitation is extended to us every time we walk up to receive his Body and his Blood.

The Body of Christ. Amen.
The Blood of Christ. Amen.

Welcome

If the group is going to share a meal or food together it would be appropriate at the beginning or end of the session or perhaps breaking the session before Prayer — eating and then ending with prayer.

Give people the opportunity to reflect briefly on last week's 'act' on the Eucharistic Prayer.

Does the variety of responses reflect different personalities or experiences, or both?

Listen to Scripture

This section helps those taking part to start to explore the session's main theme.

See notes on page xiii.

As the passage is quite long there may not be time to read it twice through. A possibility would be to have just one reading but pause for silence between each paragraph.

Listen to Scripture

Now on that same day two of them were going to a village called Emmaus, about seven miles from Jerusalem, and talking with each other about all these things that had happened. While they were talking and discussing, Jesus himself came near and went with them, but their eyes were kept from recognising him.

And he said to them, "What are you discussing with each other while you walk along?" They stood still, looking sad. Then one of them, whose name was Cleopas, answered him, "Are you the only stranger in Jerusalem who does not know the things that have taken place there in these days?" He asked them, "What things?" They replied, "The things about Jesus of Nazareth, who was a prophet mighty in deed and word before God and all the people, and how our chief priests and leaders handed him over to be condemned to death and crucified him. But we had hoped that he was the one to redeem Israel. Yes, and besides all this, it is now the third day since these things took place. Moreover, some women of our group astounded us. They were at the tomb early this morning, and when they did not find his body there, they came back and told us that they had indeed seen a vision of angels who said that he was alive. Some of those who were with us went to the tomb and found it just as the women had said; but they did not see him."

Then he said to them, "Oh, how foolish you are, and how slow of heart to believe all that the prophets have declared! Was it not necessary that the Messiah should suffer these things and then enter into his glory?" Then beginning with Moses and all the prophets, he interpreted to them the things about himself in all the scriptures.

As they came near the village to which they were going, he walked ahead as if he were going on. But they urged him strongly, saying, "Stay with us, because it is almost evening and the day is now nearly over." So he went in to stay with them.

When he was at the table with them, he took bread, blessed and broke it, and gave it to them. Then their eyes were opened, and they recognised him; and he vanished from their sight. They said to each other, "Were not our hearts burning within us while he was talking to us on the road, while he was opening the scriptures to us?"

That same hour they got up and returned to Jerusalem; and they found the eleven and their companions gathered together. They were saying, "The Lord has risen indeed, and he has appeared to Simon!" Then they told what had happened on the road, and how he had been made known to them in the breaking of the bread.

Luke 24: 13–35

Our Experience

- What is it like to share your story with someone?
- What is it like to share a meal with someone?

....

....

....

....

....

....

....

....

....

....

....

....

....

....

What is it like to share your story with someone?

Possible responses

- It opens us to relationship.
- It is an act of trust.
- It can leave us vulnerable.
- Sense of vulnerability and trust
- Care and commitment
- New beginning
- It can be a relief
- To articulate and gain sense of perspective

Possible supplementary questions

- What are the stories that unite us as a Church, as a parish or as a group?

What is it like to share a meal with someone?

Possible responses

- It can be a special occasion
- Sign of love
- Intimacy
- Commitment
- Companionship
- To be host/guest is special
- Heart warming

Possible supplementary questions

- How is this different from just eating at the same time as other people?

Read & Reflect

How does the Breaking of Bread reveal Christ?

Possible responses

- His broken body shared by all
- Breaking is sign of sacrifice
- Sign of sharing — many parts of one body
- Self giving — holding nothing back

Possible supplementary questions:

- Does the breaking matter?
- Is this a significant moment in our parish's celebration of Mass?

Read & Reflect

CELEBRATING THE MASS

Communion Rite

200. The eating and drinking together of the Lord's Body and Blood in a Paschal meal is the culmination of the Eucharist. The assembly is made ready to share in this banquet by a series of rites that lead from the Eucharistic Prayer directly to the Communion. The themes underlying these rites are the mutual love and reconciliation that are both the condition and the fruit of worthy communion and the unity of the many in the one. These themes are symbolised at both the natural and the sacramental level in the signs of bread and wine now become the Body and Blood of Christ.

- Though each of these rites (the Lord's Prayer, Sign of Peace, Breaking of the Bread) is important in itself, in the context of the whole celebration they constitute together a transition from one high point, the Eucharistic Prayer, to another, the sharing in Communion…

Breaking of the Bread (Fraction)

205. This characteristic action of Christ at the feeding of the multitude, at the Last Supper, and at his meals with the disciples after his resurrection was so central to the Eucharist that it seems to have given its name to the entire celebration in the days of the Apostles. The natural, the practical, the symbolic, and the spiritual are all inextricably linked in this most powerful symbol. Just as many grains of wheat are ground, kneaded, and baked together to become one loaf, which is then broken and shared out among many to bring them into one table-fellowship, so those gathered are made one body in the one bread of life which is Christ (see 1 Corinthians 10:17).

206. In order for the meaning of this symbolism to be perceived, both the bread and the breaking must be truly authentic and recognisable. The eucharistic Bread is to "have the appearance of food" and is to be made so that it is able to be broken and distributed to at least some of the members of the assembly…

Distribution of Communion

209. Faithful to the Lord's command to his disciples to "Take and eat," "Take and drink," the assembly completes the Eucharistic action by together eating and drinking the elements consecrated during the celebration. It is most desirable that the faithful share the chalice. Drinking at the Eucharist is a sharing in the sign of the new covenant (see Luke 22:20), a foretaste of the heavenly banquet (see Matthew 26:29), a sign of participation in the suffering Christ (see Mark 10:38-39).

210. The Communion procession expresses the humble patience of the poor moving forward to be fed, the alert expectancy of God's people sharing the Paschal meal in readiness for their journey, the joyful confidence of God's people on the march toward the promised land. In England and Wales it is through this action of walking solemnly in procession that the faithful make their sign of reverence in preparation for receiving Communion.

For Discussion

- How does the Breaking of Bread reveal Christ?
- In what ways do we express unity with Christ and with each other in the Communion Rite?
- What helps/hinders our celebration of Communion?

....
....
....
....
....
....
....
....
....
....
....
....
....

In what ways do we express unity with Christ and with each other in the Communion Rite?

Possible responses

- Praying Lord's Prayer together
- Sharing Sign of Peace
- Processing to Communion in a reverent manner
- Receiving Communion
- Saying 'Amen'
- Singing Communion Song
- Silence after Communion
- Taking Communion to sick and housebound

Possible supplementary questions…

Continue with next question

What helps/hinders our celebration of Communion?

Possible responses

- See answers to second question for 'helps'
- Pushing and shoving in queue
- Not receiving from chalice
- Sense of rush
- Music that stops me praying
- Lack of reverence

Possible supplementary questions:

- What is our response to receiving communion?

Act

Act

- See whether your journal notes on the Sunday scriptures help you to recognise Christ's presence in your daily living.

- Where have you had the opportunity to be Christ for others?

Prayer

The whole community devoted themselves to the apostles' teaching and fellowship, to the breaking of bread and the prayers. Awe came upon everyone, because many wonders and signs were being done by the apostles. All who believed were together and had all things in common; they would sell their possessions and goods and distribute the proceeds to all, as any had need. Day by day, as they spent much time together in the temple, they broke bread at home and ate their food with glad and generous hearts, praising God and having the goodwill of all the people. And day by day the Lord added to their number those who were being saved.

Acts 2: 42–47

We thank you, Father,
for the holy vine of David, your servant,
which you have revealed through Jesus, your Son.
  Praise to you now and evermore!

We thank you, Father,
for the life and the knowledge
that you have revealed through Jesus, your Son.
  Praise to you now and evermore!

Just as this bread that we break
  was once distributed on a hillside
and its fragments gathered so as not to lose any,
so let your Church be gathered
from the farthest parts of the earth into your Kingdom.
  Praise to you now and evermore!

Because yours are the glory and the power forever.
  Praise to you now and evermore!

We thank you, holy Father,
for your holy name that dwells in our hearts.
Praise to you now and evermore!

For the knowledge, the faith, and the immortality
that you have revealed to us through Jesus, your Son.
Praise to you now and evermore!

It is you, all-powerful Master, who created the universe
in praise of your name.
Praise to you now and evermore!

To all you give food and drink;
but to us you give the grace of a spiritual food,
of a drink for eternal life through Jesus, your Son.
Praise to you now and evermore!

Above all, we thank you for your power.
Praise to you now and evermore!

Remember, Lord, your Church,
deliver it from every evil,
and make it perfect in your love.
Praise to you now and evermore!

Gather together from the four winds
this sanctified Church
into the kingdom that you have prepared.
Praise to you now and evermore!

Come, Lord, and let this world pass!
Amen.

Hosanna to the house of David!
Amen.

Let him who is holy come!
Amen.

Let him who is not, repent!
Amen.

Maranatha — Come, Lord!
Amen.

Lucien Deiss
based on the Didache

Prayer
*See section in Introduction
(page xvi).*

Gather

- Light a candle(s) and/or time
of silence:
*In the name of the Father…
Let us begin our time of prayer
with a few moments silence.*

- Sing a song or chant about
Communion, unity in Christ.

Listen

- Acts 2:42–47
*Because we are in communion
with him we are in communion
with each other.*

Respond

- Time of silent reflection

- Use text from **Didache**
Either read antiphonally
(in two groups)
or responsorially
(everyone says or sings the
refrain).

Sending Forth

- Leader:
*The Lord bless us,
and keep us from all evil,
and bring us to everlasting life.*
All: Amen

For next week

*Prepare photocopies of the
Participant's Feedback forms
(page 75) for distributing to
group members at the next
meeting.*

Further Reading

CELEBRATING THE MASS

Bread and Wine

107. The very nature of sacramental symbolism demands that the elements for the Eucharist be recognisable, in themselves and without explanation, as food and drink.

- Bread must be recently baked, made only from wheat flour, and should have the appearance of food. In colour, taste, texture, and smell it should be identifiable as bread by those who are to share it.

- It is therefore expedient that the eucharistic bread, even though unleavened and baked in the traditional shape, be made in such a way that the priest at Mass with a congregation is able in practice to break it into parts for distribution to at least some of the faithful. Small hosts are, however, in no way ruled out when the number of those receiving Holy Communion or other pastoral needs require it. The action of the fraction or breaking of bread, which gave its name to the Eucharist in apostolic times, will bring out more clearly the force and importance of the sign of unity of all in the one bread, and of the sign of charity by the fact that the one bread is distributed among the brothers and sisters.

- Wine should be natural and pure, from the fruit of the grape, and free from any foreign substance. To be seen and recognised for what it is and what it signifies, it can help greatly if the wine is brought to the altar in clear glass containers and is of a sufficiently rich colour to be clearly distinguishable from water.

- Care should be taken to ensure that the bread and the wine for the Eucharist are kept fresh; that the wine does not sour or the bread spoil or become too hard to be broken easily.

- In parishes where there is a ministry of baking the Eucharistic bread for the community, care should be taken to observe the canonical requirement that plain wheat flour and water only should be used. (Recipes for baking bread for the Eucharist are available on the Liturgy Office website.) Where there are vineyards within the parish, deanery or diocesan boundaries, "fruit of the vine and work of human hands" can take on an enhanced meaning when the wine used has been produced in the locality.

Communion Rite

200. The eating and drinking together of the Lord's Body and Blood in a Paschal meal is the culmination of the Eucharist. The assembly is made ready to share in this banquet by a series of rites that lead from the Eucharistic Prayer directly to the Communion. The themes underlying these rites are the mutual love and reconciliation that are both the condition and the fruit of worthy communion and the unity of the many in the one. These themes are symbolised at both the natural and the sacramental level in the signs of bread and wine now become the Body and Blood of Christ.

- Though each of these rites (the Lord's Prayer, Sign of Peace, Breaking of the Bread) is important in itself, in the context of the whole celebration they constitute together a transition from one high point, the Eucharistic Prayer, to another, the sharing in Communion. Their musical treatment should not be so elaborate as to give the impression that they are of greater significance than the giving thanks which precedes them or the eating and drinking which follows them and which is accompanied by communal song.

The Lord's Prayer

201. The community of the baptised is constituted as the family of God by the Spirit of adoption. In the fullness of this Spirit, who has once again been invoked upon it, the assembly calls on God as Father. Because of its themes of daily bread and mutual forgiveness, the Lord's Prayer has been used in all liturgical traditions as a most appropriate preparation for Communion, "so that what is holy may, in fact, be given to those who are holy." The final petition is expanded into a prayer that concludes with the congregational doxology or acclamation *For the kingdom*, which was appended to the Lord's Prayer in some of the earliest liturgical texts and in texts of the New Testament.

- As the family prayer of all God's children, the Lord's Prayer belongs to the whole assembly. When sung, the setting chosen should be capable of being sung by all present. In this case, it will normally be desirable for the priest to sing the embolism that follows and for the priest and people together to sing the concluding acclamation *For the kingdom*. If it is not possible for the priest to sing the embolism, a spoken embolism may be accompanied by quiet instrumental underpinning, leading directly into the assembly's concluding acclamation.

The Rite of Peace

202. A ritual kiss is mentioned in the oldest writings of the New Testament and is found in the Eucharistic liturgy from the earliest days of the Church (see Romans 16:16). In most traditions it occurs before the Presentation of Gifts and is understood as a manifestation of that mutual love and reconciliation that Jesus called for before the offering of sacrifice (see Matthew 5:23). Eventually in the Roman tradition it found its place after the Lord's Prayer, whose themes of mutual forgiveness it echoes. In the early Church it was described as a "seal" placed on prayer.

203. The biblical concept of peace includes total well-being, a life in harmony with God and with ourselves, with our neighbours and with the whole of creation. Such peace can only be the pure gift of God. It is won for us by the risen Christ, present in the midst of the assembly, and so it is the peace of Christ that is exchanged.

204. The exchange of peace prior to the reception of Communion is an acknowledgement that Christ whom we receive in the Sacrament is already present in our neighbour. In this exchange the assembly acknowledges the insistent Gospel truth that communion with God in Christ is enjoyed in communion with our sisters and brothers in Christ. The rite of peace is not an expression merely of human solidarity or good will; it is rather an opening of ourselves and our neighbours to a challenge and a gift from beyond ourselves. Like the *Amen* at Communion, it is the acceptance of a challenge, a profession of faith that we are members, one with another, in the body of Christ.

  • The peace is always exchanged, though the invitation which introduces it is optional.

  • In England and Wales the customary sign is a handshake, however, it is important that this is not seen simply as a greeting but as expressing peace, communion and charity. A handclasp may be a more authentic sign than the customary handshake.

  • All the members of the assembly, ministers and people, turn to those immediately around them. It is not transmitted in sequence, as it were from a single source. Christ, who is its only source, is present and active in the assembly.

  • The sign is sufficiently strong and expressive in itself not to need explanatory song or commentary.

Breaking of the Bread (Fraction)

205. This characteristic action of Christ at the feeding of the multitude, at the Last Supper, and at his meals with the disciples after his resurrection was so central to the Eucharist that it seems to have given its name to the entire celebration in the days of the Apostles. The natural, the practical, the symbolic, and the spiritual are all inextricably linked in this most powerful symbol. Just as many grains of wheat are ground, kneaded, and baked together to become one loaf, which is then broken and shared out among many to bring them into one table-fellowship, so those gathered are made one body in the one bread of life which is Christ (see 1 Corinthians 10:17).

206. In order for the meaning of this symbolism to be perceived, both the bread and the breaking must be truly authentic and recognisable. The eucharistic Bread is to "have the appearance of food" and is to be made so that it is able to be broken and distributed to at least some of the members of the assembly.

   • During the Breaking of the Bread, the *Agnus Dei* is sung or said. The assembly calls on Jesus as the Lamb of God (see John 1:29, 36) who has conquered sin and death (see 1 Peter 1:18; Book of Revelation 5:6, 13:8). The *Agnus Dei* is a litany-song intended to accompany the action of breaking and may therefore be prolonged by repetition. It loses its entire purpose if a perfunctory Breaking of Bread is already completed before the *Agnus Dei* has even begun.

Communion

Private Preparation of the Priest

207. The prayer for the private preparation of the priest is recited inaudibly. At this time the faithful prepare themselves quietly and in their own way for Communion.

Invitation to Communion

208. The consecrated elements, the Lord's Body and Blood, are raised up and shown to the people in a gesture that is inviting but dignified. The congregation is invited to Communion with words that express the confidence of the baptised and to which they respond with the humility of the centurion (see Matthew 8:9).

Distribution of Communion

209. Faithful to the Lord's command to his disciples to "Take and eat," "Take and drink," the assembly completes the Eucharistic action by eating and drinking together the elements consecrated during the celebration. Also for this reason, it is most desirable that the

faithful share the chalice. Drinking at the Eucharist is a sharing in the sign of the new covenant (see Luke 22:20), a foretaste of the heavenly banquet (see Matthew 26:29), a sign of participation in the suffering Christ (see Mark 10:38-39). In accord with the conditions laid down by the Conference of Bishops provision should be made for this fullest form of participation.

210. The Communion procession expresses the humble patience of the poor moving forward to be fed, the alert expectancy of God's people sharing the Paschal meal in readiness for their journey, the joyful confidence of God's people on the march toward the promised land. In England and Wales it is through this action of walking solemnly in procession that the faithful make their sign of reverence in preparation for receiving Communion.

211. All signs of discrimination or distinctions among persons at the Lord's table are to be avoided.

Blessings and Spiritual Communion

212. Even though some in the assembly may not receive 'sacramental' Communion, all are united in some way by the Holy Spirit. The traditional idea of 'spiritual' Communion is an important one to remember and reaffirm. The invitation often given at Mass to those who may not receive sacramental Communion — for example, children before their First Communion and adults who are not Catholics — to receive a 'blessing' at the moment of Communion emphasises that a deep spiritual communion is possible even when we do not share together the Sacrament of the Body and Blood of Christ.

Communion Song

213. The Communion of priest and people is helpfully accompanied by prayerful congregational song. This singing is meant to express the communicants' union in spirit by means of the unity of their voices, to give evidence of joy of heart, and to highlight more the "communitarian" nature of the Communion procession. The Roman Rite provides an antiphon to be sung at this point. The antiphon may be replaced by a psalm or suitable liturgical song. The text and the music should be suited to the mystery being celebrated, the part of the Mass, the liturgical season or the day. The singing continues for as long as the faithful are receiving the Sacrament. If, however, there is to be a hymn after Communion, the Communion chant should be ended at the right time.

Period of Silence or Song of Praise

215. When Communion is completed, the whole assembly may observe a period of total silence. In the absence of all words, actions,

music, or movement, a moment of deep corporate stillness and contemplation may be experienced. Such silence is important to the rhythm of the whole celebration and is welcome in a busy and restless world.

- Silence and true stillness can be achieved if all, the assembly and its ministers, take part in it.

- As an alternative or addition to silent contemplation, a psalm or song of praise may be sung. Since there should normally have been singing during Communion, silence may be more desirable.

- This period of deep and tranquil communion is not to be interrupted even by parish announcements, which if needed come correctly on the Concluding Rite, or the taking of a collection. Nor should this silence be broken or overlaid by the public reading of devotional material.

Prayer after Communion
216. In a final presidential prayer that brings to a close the Communion Rite, the community of faith asks that the spiritual effects of the Eucharist be experienced in its members' lives.

Before you begin

Read through the session.

Look over the questions — how would you answer them?

Does anything in particular strike you; something you have not thought of before; something you disagree with; something you want more time to think about.

It is unlikely that your group will have the same response as you nor it is desirable that they should but it is important that you are familiar with the material, understand the connection between the different parts and have an overall feel for the session.

Aim

Nourished by the word and Holy Communion we are sent forth to be Christ's body in the world.

Welcome

Listen to Scripture

Matthew 28: 16–20

The account of the Ascension contains a command and a promise. A command to make disciples of all the nations and a promise that Jesus is with us always. In Matthew's account it is introduced with the intriguing phrase that some of the disciples hesitated.

Our Experience
• What draws me to Christ? What causes me to 'hesitate'?
• What is my mission?
  What is our mission?
• What helps/hinders us committing to it?

Read & Reflect

The extracts give an overview of the Concluding Rite and make the fundamental connection between what we celebrate and how we live our lives.

For Discussion
• Why do I think Mass ends in the way that it does?
• How does the celebration of Mass show me how to live?
• In what ways are we a community outside of Sunday Mass?

Act

To consider how I can help my parish's celebration of Mass to more fully realise its potential.

Prayer

6. Mission

*Nourished by the word and Holy Communion
we are sent forth to be Christ's body in the world.*

A friend of mine, Jeanette Easley, once a lay missioner in Ecuador, wrote of an experience she once had in a restaurant.

Recently, after having dinner at an outdoor chicken restaurant in Guayaquil, we had one piece of chicken left with everyone too full too eat it. I immediately thought I would like to take it with us and give it to a beggar in the street. (This was a new thought for me; previously I would have left it.) As we were walking down the street, I saw a woman huddled in a doorway with all her worldly possessions and her five children (two months to six years old). I thought "I can't give this chicken to her. There is only one piece, and there are six of them.

The words of Jesus flashed in my mind and I went over to the family, knelt down, introduced myself, offered what I had and was welcomed by warmness and cheer. We talked a few minutes and then prayed together. The woman ended up giving me her blessing and the kids thanked me and kissed me. I don't know what happened after I left, who ate the chicken but I knew beyond a doubt that God's grace was enough.

As Christians we must reflect Christ. United as the Body of Christ, in community support, we can start transforming our world were we live, with the little we have, in the love, grace, and power of the Spirit. In many ways I have been ignoring the reality of grace and making excuses why I don't do anything, saying "what little I have won't change their situation". What I have realized lately, is that I was reacting at a very human level and making human comparisons instead of faith.

Let us go in peace to love and serve the Lord.
Thanks be to God.

Welcome

Spend some time sharing on last week's action.

Have you thought of being in communion in a different way?

Listen to Scripture

This section helps those taking part to start to explore the session's main theme.

See notes on page xiii.

What draws me to Christ? What causes me to 'hesitate'?

Possible responses

- Obligation
- Acceptance
- Forgiveness
- Promise of eternal life
- Resurrection
- Christ calls us.
- Mary points to her Son
- The demands of our mission
- And is it true?
- What will other people think?
- Do I have to believe all of this?

Possible supplementary questions:

- Why do you think some of the disciples hesitated?

Listen to Scripture

The eleven disciples set out for Galilee,
to the mountain
where Jesus had arranged to meet them.
When they saw him they fell down before him,
though some hesitated.

Jesus came up and spoke to them.
He said, 'All authority in heaven and on earth
has been given to me.
Go, therefore, make disciples of all the nations;
baptise them in the name of the Father and of the Son
and of the Holy Spirit,
and teach them to observe all the commands I gave you.
And know that I am with you always;
yes, to the end of time.'

Matthew 28: 16–20

Our Experience

- What draws me to Christ? What causes me to 'hesitate'?

- What is my mission?
  What is our mission?

- What helps/hinders us committing to it?

....
....
....
....
....
....
....
....
....
....
....
....
....
....
....
....
....
....

**What is my mission?
What is our mission?**

Possible responses

- To do good
- To help others
- To be Christ in the world
- To build up the Body of Christ
- To proclaim Good News to the poor

Possible supplementary questions:
Continue with next question

What helps/hinders us committing to it?

Possible responses

- Example of others
- Too busy
- Understanding that all we do can build up the Body of Christ
- Thinking I have to do lots of other things

Possible supplementary questions:

- Does it come down to attitude? Is it how we do things rather than the things that we do?

Read & Reflect

Read & Reflect

Why do I think Mass ends in the way that it does?

Possible responses

- To remind us why we are at Mass
- To remind us we are sent out with a common purpose
- The announcements remind us that there is more to being Church than coming to Mass
- To remind us that Christ is with us
- Sense of urgency

Possible supplementary questions:

- Can you remember any particular times when you left with a strong sense of mission — to be sent out to love and serve the world?

How does the celebration of Mass show me how to live?

Possible responses

- Live as member of God's people
- To listen to God's word
- To be grateful
- To be in communion
- To be given a purpose

Possible supplementary questions:

- Why do we need to do these things again and again?

Read & Reflect

CELEBRATING THE MASS

217. After the Communion Rite, the Mass closes with a brief Concluding Rite. Its purpose is to send the people forth to put into effect in their daily lives the Paschal Mystery and the unity in Christ which they have celebrated. They are given a sense of abiding mission, which calls them to witness to Christ in the world and to bring the Gospel to the poor.

CONSTITUTION ON THE SACRED LITURGY

9. The liturgy does not exhaust the entire activity of the Church. Before people can come to the liturgy they must be called to faith and to conversion…

   Therefore the Church announces the good tidings of salvation to those who do not believe, so that all may know the true God and Jesus Christ whom he has sent, and may be converted from their ways, doing penance. To believers, also, the Church must ever preach faith and penance, prepare them for the sacraments, teach them to observe all that Christ has commanded, and invite them to all the works of charity, worship, and the apostolate. For all these works make it clear that Christ's faithful, though not of this world, are to be the light of the world and to glorify the Father in the eyes of all.

10. Still, the liturgy is the summit toward which the activity of the Church is directed; at the same time it is the fount from which all the Church's power flows. For the aim and object of apostolic works is that all who are made children of God by faith and baptism should come together to praise God in the midst of his Church, to take part in the sacrifice, and to eat the Lord's supper.

    The liturgy in its turn moves the faithful, filled with "the paschal sacraments", to be "one in holiness"; it prays that "they may hold fast in their lives to what they have grasped by their faith"; the renewal in the eucharist of the covenant between the Lord and his people draws the faithful into the compelling love of Christ and sets them on fire. From the liturgy, therefore, and especially from the eucharist, grace is poured forth upon us as from a fountain; the liturgy is the source for achieving in the most effective way possible human sanctification and God's glorification, the end to which all the Church's activities are directed.

For Discussion

- Why do I think Mass ends in the way that it does?

- How does the celebration of Mass show me how to live?

- In what ways are we a community outside of Sunday Mass?

In what ways are we a community outside of Sunday Mass?

Possible responses

- Social action
- In our families and our friendships
- In small groups such as this
- In school
- At the school gates
- United in prayer
- Parish social club
- Parish organisations
- Ecumenical groups

Possible supplementary questions:

- How are these drawn into our celebration of Sunday Mass?

Act

Act

- To consider how I can help my parish's celebration of Mass to more fully realise its potential.

Prayer

We declare to you what was from the beginning,
what we have heard, what we have seen with our eyes,
what we have looked at and touched with our hands,
concerning the word of life — this life was revealed,
and we have seen it and testify to it,
and declare to you the eternal life that was with the Father
and was revealed to us
— we declare to you what we have seen and heard
so that you also may have fellowship with us;
and truly our fellowship is with the Father
and with his Son Jesus Christ.
We are writing these things so that our joy may be
complete.

1 John 1: 1–4

God of glory,
whose beloved Son has shown us
that true worship comes from humble and contrite hearts:
bless all of us as we hear your call
to serve the needs of our parish.
Grant that our service may be fruitful
and our worship pleasing in your sight.

We ask this through Christ our Lord.

Amen.

Prayer

See section from Introduction (page xvi).

Gather

- Light a candle(s) and/or time of silence:
  In the name of the Father...
  Let us begin our time of prayer with a few moments silence.

- Sing a song or chant about Mission, discipleship, ministry, sending forth.

Listen

- **1 John 1: 1–14**

Respond

- Time of silent reflection
- Pray the **blessing** text

Sending Forth

- Leader:
  The Lord bless us,
  and keep us from all evil,
  and bring us to everlasting life.
  All: *Amen*

Further Reading

CONSTITUTION ON THE SACRED LITURGY

9. The liturgy does not exhaust the entire activity of the Church. Before people can come to the liturgy they must be called to faith and to conversion: "How then are they to call upon him in whom they have not yet believed? But how are they to believe him whom they have not heard? And how are they to hear if no one preaches? And how are men to preach unless they be sent?" (Rom. 10:14-15).

   Therefore the Church announces the good tidings of salvation to those who do not believe, so that all may know the true God and Jesus Christ whom he has sent, and may be converted from their ways, doing penance. To believers, also, the Church must ever preach faith and penance, prepare them for the sacraments, teach them to observe all that Christ has commanded, and invite them to all the works of charity, worship, and the apostolate. For all these works make it clear that Christ's faithful, though not of this world, are to be the light of the world and to glorify the Father in the eyes of all.

10. Still, the liturgy is the summit toward which the activity of the Church is directed; at the same time it is the fount from which all the Church's power flows. For the aim and object of apostolic works is that all who are made children of God by faith and baptism should come together to praise God in the midst of his Church, to take part in the sacrifice, and to eat the Lord's supper.

    The liturgy in its turn moves the faithful, filled with "the paschal sacraments," to be "one in holiness"; it prays that "they may hold fast in their lives to what they have grasped by their faith"; the renewal in the eucharist of the covenant between the Lord and his people draws the faithful into the compelling love of Christ and sets them on fire. From the liturgy, therefore, and especially from the eucharist, grace is poured forth upon us as from a fountain; the liturgy is the source for achieving in the most effective way possible human sanctification and God's glorification, the end to which all the Church's activities are directed.

11. But in order that the liturgy may possess its full effectiveness, it is necessary that the faithful come to it with proper dispositions, that their minds should be attuned to their voices, and that they should cooperate with divine grace, lest they receive it in vain. Pastors must therefore realise that when the liturgy is celebrated, something more is required than the mere observation of the laws governing valid and lawful celebration; it is also their duty to ensure that the faithful take part fully aware of what they are

doing, actively engaged in the rite, and enriched by its effects.

12. The spiritual life, however, is not limited solely to participation in the liturgy. Christians are indeed called to pray in union with each other, but they must also enter into their chamber to pray to the Father in secret; further, according to the teaching of the Apostle, they should pray without ceasing. We learn from the same Apostle that we must always bear about in our body the dying of Jesus, so that the life also of Jesus may be made manifest in our bodily frame. This is why we ask the Lord in the sacrifice of the Mass that, "receiving the offering of the spiritual victim," he may fashion us for himself "as an eternal gift".

CELEBRATING THE MASS

Concluding Rite

217. After the Communion Rite, the Mass closes with a brief Concluding Rite. Its purpose is to send the people forth to put into effect in their daily lives the Paschal Mystery and the unity in Christ which they have celebrated. They are given a sense of abiding mission, which calls them to witness to Christ in the world and to bring the Gospel to the poor.

218. The Concluding Rite consists of

- brief announcements, if they are necessary.

- the priest's greeting and blessing, which on certain days and occasions is enriched and expressed in the Prayer over the People or another more solemn formula.

- the dismissal of the people by the deacon or the priest, so that each member goes out to do good works, praising and blessing God.

- the kissing of the altar by the priest and the deacon, followed by a profound bow to the altar by the priest, the deacon, and the other ministers, If there is a tabernacle containing the Most Blessed Sacrament on the sanctuary, they genuflect.

- an orderly procession of the ministers and the assembly.

- When another liturgical rite is to follow immediately, for example, the final commendation at a funeral, the entire concluding rite is omitted because these other rites will have their own form of conclusion.

Announcements

219. Just as the introductory comments by the priest at the beginning of the celebration may help the assembly to a better appreciation and experience of the mysteries celebrated in the Eucharist, so also the pastoral announcements at the end may help the people make the transition from worship into renewed Christian witness in society. They should help people become aware of the faith life and pastoral activity of the community and invite participation in the ongoing work of the Church.

Dismissal of Commissioned Ministers taking Communion to the Housebound or Sick

220. It is fitting for Holy Communion to be taken directly from Mass to the sick or those unable to leave their homes.

- Appropriate times for the deacons, acolytes, or commissioned ministers of Holy Communion to receive a pyx from the priest and be 'sent' to take Holy Communion and leave the assembly are either after the Communion of the people or immediately before the final blessing.

- The ministers may depart before the Prayer after Communion prayer, immediately after the Prayer after Communion or as part of the concluding procession of ministers.

- Local circumstances will determine which of these various options will be most fitting in any particular parish.

221. The Presider will normally speak words of dismissal or missioning over the ministers taking Holy Communion to the sick and housebound. These words may be based on the words of the Communion antiphon, on the readings of the day, or in a simple form such as:

> *Go now, to our sisters and brothers*
> *unable to be with us for reasons of sickness and infirmity.*

> *Take to them from our celebration*
> *the word of God and Holy Communion,*
> *that they might share with us*
> *these signs of the Lord's goodness.*

Greeting

222. The greeting *The Lord be with you* helps the assembly to focus attention again on the prayerful aspect of the blessing.

Blessing

223. As Scripture attests, all beings are created and kept in existence by God's gracious goodness. They are themselves blessings from God and should move us to bless God in return. This is above all true since the Word has come in flesh to make all things holy by the mystery of the incarnation.

224. Blessings, therefore, refer first and foremost to God, whose majesty and goodness they extol, and they involve human beings, whom God governs and by divine providence protects.

Dismissal

225. The Dismissal sends the members of the congregation forth to praise and bless the Lord in the midst of their daily responsibilities.

Participant's feedback form

This form is for giving out in Session 6. It is intended to provide both feedback on the meetings to the parish and to give people the opportunity to offer their services to the parish community.

Copies for the group will need to be made before the session. The parish will normally provide copies for you. It can also be downloaded from the Liturgy Office website [www.liturgyoffice.org.uk/Resources]. Copies will need to be returned to the parish — you may be asked to bring them to a final session for group leaders (see page 88).

Further Reading

Other writings on the Mass and the Liturgy more generally include:

The *Catechism of the Catholic Church* (Part Two. The Celebration of the Christian Mystery, paragraphs 1066- 1690)

Pope John Paul II. *Spiritus et Sponsa*. London, CTS, 2003

Pope John Paul II. *Ecclesia de Eucharistia*. London, CTS, 2003

The Liturgy Office website provides a wide range of resources and information — www.liturgyoffice.org.uk. Including material on the *General Instruction* and *Celebrating the Mass*.

Of particular interest will be the *Liturgy Newsletter*, published four times a year which is distributed to each diocese for circulation. It can be downloaded from the website.

A subscription service to English language liturgical periodicals published overseas is available. Some of these are technical and scholarly journals; others are more popular and easily accessible, for example *Assembly*, *Catechumenate* and *Liturgy News*. Further details of these publications and the subscription service can be found on the website together with details of UK journals such as *Music and Liturgy* of the Society of St Gregory.

With Hearts & Minds
Participant's feedback form

In completing your form, please remember the agreement to confidentiality made by your group. Only make a note of things that are your own thoughts and reactions.

What are the good things that you remember from your group's meetings?

....

....

....

....

....

Were there any particular things that you found difficult or challenging?

....

....

....

....

....

Are there any particular issues that you would like the parish community to take up and consider?

....

....

....

....

....

With Hearts and Minds

Are there any particular ways in which you would like to offer your services to the parish community? Opportunities include:

Liturgy Group ☐
a group sharing in the responsibility for long term planning with regard to the parish's liturgical formation, and celebration of the liturgy

Music Ministry ☐
as member of choir or music group, musician, cantor

Liturgy Planning Group ☐
a group helping to prepare the liturgies for a particular week or season

Minister of Holy Communion ☐
as member of team assisting in taking Holy Communion to the housebound or sick, and in helping to distribute Holy Communion at Mass

Ministry of Word ☐
part of a team of readers, preparers of intercessions, collaborating with Catechists

Ministry of Welcome ☐
as member of team that helps ensure that everyone coming to the Church is helped

I would be interested in learning more about...
(tick a box or use the space below)

....

....

....

Is there some work not mentioned above that you would be interested in?

....

....

....

Are there any further comments you would like to make about the groups and the work they have been doing over the past weeks?

....

....

....

Name: ....

Address: ....

....

Telephone Number: .... Email address: ....

I give my consent for these details to be retained by the parish, and entered on any database maintained by the office. They should not be passed to those outside the parish, without my consent.

Glossary

SESSION 1 INTRODUCTION

In main text

Liturgy: the official worship of the Church. The Liturgy includes Mass, but also other celebrations such as Baptism and Confirmation, Morning and Evening Prayer. Other forms of prayer together, such as Stations of the Cross and the Rosary have their own important place in the devotional life of the Church.

In Further reading

Paschal Mystery: An equivalent term would be 'Easter Mystery'. The phrase refers to the whole event of the passion, death, and resurrection of Jesus Christ.

The word 'Paschal' comes from the Greek Word for Passover. In the liturgies of the Triduum (the Mass of the Lord's Supper on Holy Thursday, the Solemn Liturgy of Good Friday and the great Vigil of Saturday night) we remember the Passover events of Israel's liberation from slavery. These provide a first echoing of the freedom from sin and death won by Jesus Christ. The language of Passover was readily applied to Jesus and what he accomplished through his faithfulness, his dying and his rising.

The word 'mystery' comes from the Greek word for 'secret reality'. It is used in many ways by the Church, for example to describe the saving life, death and resurrection of Jesus, but also to describe the rites in which we remember and engage with these events. "As we prepare to celebrate these sacred mysteries…" are probably familiar words to us all. In each case the use of the word reminds us that there is more involved here than what immediately meets the eye.

Session 2 Gathering

In main text

A royal priesthood: the sole priesthood in the Church is Christ's. It is shared in by all those who have been baptised. In baptism, in Christ, we become "a chosen race, a royal priesthood, a holy nation, God's own people" (1 Pt 2:9). The 'royal priesthood' or 'baptismal priesthood' is exercised for the salvation of the world, "that you may proclaim the mighty acts of him who called you out of darkness into his marvellous light." (1 Pt 2:9).

Those of the baptised who have been ordained as priest or bishop share in Christ's priesthood also through the sacrament of orders. This 'ministerial priesthood' is especially exercised for the benefit of the Church, in the preaching of the word and in presiding at the celebration of the sacraments.

memorial: Key to all Christian liturgy is a work of remembering that finds its natural expression in the act of thanksgiving. The remembering is not 'just' an act of memory, but a new participation in the present reality of Christ's saving love.

SESSION 3 WORD

In main text

Prayer of the Faithful (general intercessions) More popularly these are called the Bidding Prayers. The Prayer of the Faithful begins with the priest calling the whole assembly to prayer. Then the deacon or reader reads each of the 'biddings' or intercessions in turn. They are addressed to the assembly, inviting them to pray to God for the named intentions. "Let us pray for…" Each intention is read out and then there is a time for people to pray silently, as asked. The silent prayer is gathered together in the response. After the final response, the priest concludes the time of prayer, with a summary prayer or collect.

Lectionary The Lectionary is the book with the series of readings for each of the days of the year. In the edition approved for use in England and Wales there are 3 volumes to the Lectionary, one for Masses on Sundays and during the Seasons, one for Masses of Weekdays in Ordinary Time (ie the numbered weeks of the year), and one for other celebrations, for example of other sacraments and for funerals.

In Further reading

Apocalyptic: The word comes from the Greek term meaning revelation or unveiling. The apocalyptic writings in the Bible include the Book of Daniel (with its visions of the Son of Man), or the Book of the Apocalypse (or Book of Revelation). In all these writings rich and complex series of images are offered which give a symbolic account of God's saving power at work in the world.

SESSION 4 THANKSGIVING

In main text

Memorial: see Session 2 page 78.

Priest celebrant: The Catechism of the Catholic Church teaches that *the* celebrant of the Church's liturgy is Christ (CCC 1136), the whole Christ, body and head. The body is the community of the baptised, the head is the glorified Christ. Whenever the body gathers for liturgical prayer, someone presides at that gathering, representing and reminding those present of the headship of Christ. When Mass is celebrated, the presider is necessarily a bishop or a priest.

In Further reading

Epiclesis: This technical word comes from the Greek, and means 'invoking' or 'calling down'. There are two such epicleses in the 'new' Eucharistic prayers – one calling on the Holy Spirit for the transformation of the bread and wine into the Body and Blood of Christ, the second calling on the Spirit to transform those who receive the sacramental food and drink into the Body of Christ, perfectly united with him.

Anamnesis: The Greek word for 'remembering' or 'memorial'.

Doxology: The word again comes from the Greek, and is formed from the Greek words for 'word' and for 'glory'. Most of our prayers end with words which offer glory to God: for example, "Glory be to the Father and to the Son and to the Holy Spirit…" The Doxology in the Eucharistic Prayer begins with the priest's words: "Through him, with him, in him…" and is answered by the Great Amen, the congregation's concluding acclamation to the Eucharistic Prayer.

Appendix

Gathering the Leaders

A Session for group leaders before you begin — usually led by the parish team.

Review and Planning for the Future

A Session for group leaders when group meetings have ended.

Gathering the Leaders

To familiarise the group leaders with their particular tasks
To give them experience of the process for each session
To give them confidence for their task

Listen to Scripture

If there is any encouragement in Christ,
any consolation from love,
any sharing in the Spirit, any compassion and sympathy,
make my joy complete:
be of the same mind, having the same love,
being in full accord and of one mind.
Do nothing from selfish ambition or conceit,
but in humility regard others as better than yourselves.
Let each of you look not to your own interests,
but to the interests of others.

Let the same mind be in you that was in Christ Jesus,
who, though he was in the form of God,
did not regard equality with God
as something to be exploited,
but emptied himself, taking the form of a slave,
being born in human likeness.
And being found in human form,
he humbled himself
and became obedient to the point of death
— even death on a cross.
Therefore God also highly exalted him
and gave him the name that is above every name,
so that at the name of Jesus every knee should bend,
in heaven and on earth and under the earth,
and every tongue should confess that Jesus Christ is Lord,
to the glory of God the Father.

Philippians 2: 1-11

Our Experience

- Can I name examples of service that I have benefited from down the years? What made these stand out?

- What is there about Christ that inspires me to live as a member of his Body, the Church?

....

....

....

....

....

....

....

....

....

....

....

....

....

....

....

....

....

....

Read & Reflect

GAUDIUM ET SPES

Vatican Council II: Pastoral Constitution on the Church in the world today.

1. The joys and hopes and the sorrows and the anxieties of people today, especially those who are poor and afflicted, are also the joys and hopes, sorrows and anxieties of the disciples of Christ, and there is nothing truly human which does not also affect them. Their community is composed of people united in Christ who are directed by the holy Spirit in their pilgrimage to the Father's kingdom and who have received the message of salvation to be communicated to everyone. For this reason it feels itself closely linked to the human race and its history.

3. …The church is not motivated by any earthly considerations, but has in mind only, with the guidance of the Paraclete, to continue the work of Christ who came into the world to give witness to the truth, to save and not to judge, to serve and to be served.

4. To discharge this function, the church has the duty in every age of examining the signs of the times and interpreting them in the light of the gospel, so that it can offer in a manner appropriate to each generation replies to the continual human questionings on the meaning of this life and the life to come and on how they are related. There is a need, then, to be aware of, and to understand, the world in which we live, together with its expectations, its desires and its frequently dramatic character…

GENERAL INSTRUCTION OF THE ROMAN MISSAL

95. In the celebration of Mass the faithful form a holy people, a people whom God has made his own, a royal priesthood, so that they may give thanks to God and offer the spotless Victim not only through the hands of the priest but also together with him, and so that they may learn to offer themselves. They should, moreover, endeavour to make this clear by their deep religious sense and their charity toward brothers and sisters who participate with them in the same celebration.

    Thus, they are to shun any appearance of individualism or division, keeping before their eyes that they have only one Father in heaven and accordingly are all brothers and sisters to each other.

96. Indeed, they form one body, whether by hearing the word of God, or by joining in the prayers and the singing, or above all by the common offering of Sacrifice and by a common partaking at the Lord's table. This unity is beautifully apparent from the gestures and postures observed in common by the faithful.

97. The faithful, moreover, should not refuse to serve the People of God gladly whenever they are asked to perform some particular ministry or role in the celebration.

For Discussion

- What helps/hinders our parish in deepening the sense of communion with Christ and with each other?

- What are my hopes for this course?
  What are my fears?

....

....

....

....

....

....

....

....

....

....

....

....

....

....

....

....

Act

- *Preparation for first meeting*
- *Use of Journals*
- *Initial reflection for Leaders*

Prayer

For this reason I bow my knees before the Father,
from whom every family in heaven
and on earth takes its name.
I pray that, according to the riches of his glory,
he may grant that you may be strengthened
in your inner being with power
through his Spirit,
and that Christ may dwell in your hearts through faith,
as you are being rooted and grounded in love.

I pray that you may have the power to comprehend,
with all the saints,
what is the breadth and length and height and depth,
and to know the love of Christ that surpasses knowledge,
so that you may be filled with all the fullness of God.
Now to him who by the power at work within us
is able to accomplish abundantly far more than all we can
ask or imagine,
to him be glory in the church and in Christ Jesus
to all generations,
forever and ever. Amen.

Ephesians 3:14-21

O God, the giver of every perfect gift,
by the grace of baptism
you adopt us as your own
and call us to your service.

Strengthen us by your Holy Spirit
to live the gospel we embrace.
Deliver us from self-seeking
and cause us to work for the common good.
Keep us loyal to Christ in all we set out to accomplish,
that the praise and the glory may be yours alone.

We ask this through our Lord Jesus Christ your Son,
who lives and reigns with you
in the unity of the Holy Spirit,
God for ever and ever.
Amen.

Review and planning for the future
final session for leaders

To reflect on the study groups
To begin to identify how the parish should follow it up.

Listen to Scripture

For as in one body we have many members,
and not all the members have the same function,
so we, who are many, are one body in Christ,
and individually we are members one of another.

We have gifts that differ according to the grace given to us:
prophecy, in proportion to faith;
ministry, in ministering; the teacher, in teaching;
the exhorter, in exhortation; the giver, in generosity;
the leader, in diligence; the compassionate, in cheerfulness.
Let love be genuine; hate what is evil,
hold fast to what is good;
love one another with mutual affection;
outdo one another in showing honour.
Do not lag in zeal, be ardent in spirit, serve the Lord.
Rejoice in hope, be patient in suffering, persevere in prayer.

Romans 12: 4–12

Our Experience

- How do we encourage and deepen the formation of those in liturgical ministry?

- In what ways can we offer on-going formation to other members of the parish?

....

....

....

....

....

....

....

....

....

....

....

....

....

....

....

....

....

....

Reflection on Experience

- In this final session time is given to reflect on the process and the feedback that has been given.

For Discussion

- For the leaders what was good about the time with the groups?
  What was more difficult?

- What are the common themes and issues that are in the feedback?

....
....
....
....
....
....
....
....
....
....
....
....
....
....
....

Act

- Prioritise the responses.
  What are the first steps?
  Who will take them?

- Draw up recommendations for the parish team.

....

....

....

....

....

....

....

....

....

....

....

....

....

....

....

....

Prayer

The whole community devoted themselves to the apostles' teaching and fellowship, to the breaking of bread and the prayers. Awe came upon everyone, because many wonders and signs were being done by the apostles. All who believed were together and had all things in common; they would sell their possessions and goods and distribute the proceeds to all, as any had need. Day by day, as they spent much time together in the temple, they broke bread at home and ate their food with glad and generous hearts, praising God and having the goodwill of all the people. And day by day the Lord added to their number those who were being saved.

Acts 2: 42–47

God of glory,
whose beloved Son has shown us
that true worship comes from humble
   and contrite hearts:
bless all of us as we hear your call
to serve the needs of our parish.
Grant that our service may be fruitful
and our worship pleasing in your sight.

We ask this through Christ our Lord.

Amen.